BE YOUR OWN MANAGER

A CAREER HANDBOOK FOR CLASSICAL MUSICIANS

BERNHARD KERRES
BETTINA MEHNE

Tenaia Management Ltd.
LONDON, UK

Tenaia Management Ltd.
71-75 Shelton Street
Covent Garden
London, WC2H 9JQ
United Kingdom
www.be-your-own-manager.com

Book Layout ©2013 BookDesignTemplates.com

Ordering Information:

Quantity sales. Special discounts are available on quantity purchases by corporations, associations, and others. For details, contact the "Special Sales Department" at the address above.

Be Your Own Manager / Bernhard Kerres and Bettina Mehne. — 1st ed.
ISBN 978-1-54390-349-2

I enjoy teaching the next generation of great cellists. Equipping them with all the right tools as well as musical excellency is close to my heart. The book provides a much needed insight.
- Gautier Capucon, cellist and Classe d'Excellence de Violoncelle

My career depended a lot on not only playing well but also on promoting what I was doing. After having raised the funds for my CD of J.S. Bach's Goldberg Variations I contacted many labels to publish it. Luckily Telarc agreed to do so and that was a big step in my career. Even today with having a dedicated management and support from my label Sony as well as others, I do take care of many aspects of the business side of my career. A book on managing my own career would have been helpful then. I am glad that Bettina and Bernhard have undertaken it to write it.
- Simone Dinnerstein, pianist

Being a great musician is one thing. Having a great career requires the first, but also an understanding of how the business works. Thanks to Bernhard Kerres and Bettina Mehne for sharing their decades of experience in classical music for the benefit of young musicians. Their book contains the wealth of knowledge a musician needs to understand the business side of their career. I recommend this book to my musician friends.
- Valery Gergiev

Being an independent artist in today's classical world means you have an unprecedented opportunity to share your own voice. If you have complete devotion to music, iron discipline, preferably your own team - and this book - you're on the right track.
- Daniel Hope, violinist

In all my years as an artist manager, the question I get asked the most, without fail, is: "Will you represent me?" I always want to respond saying: "When you have successfully managed your own career to the point that the only way to move forward is with professional representation, you are ready for management." Artists often don't know where to start and this book is THE ANSWER for all the questions that follow! How to jump-start and manage your career, how to be your best representative, how to be an entrepreneur and build your own brand, and how to make things happen. Once an artist understands all these business aspects, they have a vital understanding of what it takes and are better poised to work effectively with managers when the time is right.
- Charlotte Lee, President and Founder of Primo Artists

"Eagerness" best describes our waiting position for the new handbook for young musicians from the dream team running Hello Stage, Bernhard & Bettina - both of whom have decades of experience in the music business. The young generation is carving out a new style of career and that calls for dynamic and flexible management. For many, the only solution is to manage their diverse portfolio careers themselves. But how? This book will show them how. We have a stash on pre-order for our talented students. Watching for the post!
- Sarah Wilson, Deputy-Chancellor, Mozarteum University

PREFACE

OVER THE PAST THREE years, we have been blessed with meeting and getting to know some of the most outstanding musicians out there in the world. HELLO STAGE (www.hellostage.com) has enabled us to meet these amazing talents after our long careers in classical music with some of its most sought after institutions, including the Wiener Konzerthaus (Vienna Concert House), The Deutsche Kammerphilharmonie Bremen, and various leading artists' managements, among others. After working with some of the greatest artists in the world, it has been such a wonderful revelation to continue to meet so many energetic and truly creative people. Thank you all for the abundance of inspiration you have given and continue to give us.

From all the time we have spent meeting with both young, but also very established musicians, we came to realize a key insight - that the business side of a classical music career is rarely taught. Most musicians learn in a process of trial-by-fire and making up their careers as they go along. We therefore thought it was time to pull together all our collective experiences and write a book addressing the many issues one might face in managing a classical music career. We hope that this book provides a lot of guidance and insight to the classical musicians of the world, as we want to contribute towards helping you build a successful career.

When using the term "musician," we mean to include everybody, from instrumentalists to singers, composers, and conductors.

There are many ways to read this book, but we'd like to share how we envisioned it. You can read it straight from beginning to end, and hopefully you will make notes in the parts you find to be relevant for where you are at in the current stage of your career. But you can also feel free to just read the chapters that you feel are most relevant to you right now, as there is no harm in that. While risking some duplication, the book is written in such a way that you can jump from one chapter to another, without reading the whole book in one go.

We have also built a website parallel to the book: www.be-your-own-manager.com. There we provide more resources, as well as a discussion forum, as it is designed to be a continuous extension to the book once this is published. We hope that you will share your thoughts and lessons from the book, suggest edits, ask questions, and provide feedback, not only for us, but also for fellow musicians. You will also be able to find dates for regular workshops we conduct at academies, conservatories, universities and other institutions, as well as sign up for our newsletter. Additionally, individual career coaching sessions can be booked on our website.

Writing a book is a journey, and as we found out, a longer one than we anticipated. We loved writing this book and truly hope you find it useful. There are many people to thank for supporting us in the process, and while we cannot mention all of them, we'd like to try to thank some:

First and foremost, this book would have never been written if it weren't for the wonderful people who worked with us to build up HELLO STAGE: Günter Lepuschitz, the technical soul behind HEL-LO STAGE; Murli Bhamidipati, who jumped into a management role in a time of need; Hanna Kristall, a wonderful musician herself; Raphael Shklarek, who managed our office in the early days; Clio Em, Nina K. Lucas, Eren Yagmuroglu, and Toygun Özdemir, who built up our social media presence; Zarin Mehta, the former President of the New York Philharmonic, who has been an advisor to HELLO STAGE almost from the start; and our board members and investors.

We also would not have started HELLO STAGE if it weren't for the encouragement of our founding members: John Axelrod, Belcea Quartet, Jasmine Choi, Steve Davislim, Martin Grubinger, Aleksey Igudesman, Hyung-ki Joo, Gabriela Montero, Ferhan & Ferzan Önder, Julian Rachlin, and Anika Vavic.

We want to thank Hartmut Höll and Jürgen Christ from the Music Academy in Karlsruhe for inviting us to talk to their students before anyone else did, as well as Ara Guzelimian for his standing invitation to speak about career management at Juilliard.

We were happily astonished by how many people supported the idea for this book by pre-ordering and participating in our crowdfunding campaign! Thank you to Maria Weiss, Mari Adachi, Hans Kerres, Gabriel Malancioiu, Coline-Marie Orliac, Sarah Wilson, Chris H. Leeb, Charlotte Lee, Leroy Yue, Antje Müller, Neilda Pacquing, Jasmine Choi, Dunka Lavrova, Andreas Neufeld, Hendrik Vanden Abeele, Stephen P. Brown, Zenaida des Aubris, Rasvan Dumitru, Maias Alyamani, Medea Bindewald, Ivan Turkalj, Christine Jasper, Giedre Chesson, Cynthia Geria Ganga, Giuseppe Mariotti, Ruth Fraser, David Hanke, Anna Carewe, BOHO Players, Dr. Helga Breuninger, Aslak Grøseth Pedersen, Trevor Williams, Aleksey Igudesman, Marie-Luise Dingler, Nareh Arghamanyan, Karina Haas, Ketevan Sharumashvili, AD Productions, Robert Rÿker, Elisa Netzer, Jacqueline Leung, Leanna Primiani, Nora Williams, Stephan Popp, Ginevra Petrucci, Jeeyoon Kim, Helena Bivar, Maria Radutu, Josep Martinez Reinoso, Elizabeth Manus, Petra Klose, Mircea Belei, Allegra Giagu, Christian Capocaccia, Heike Matthiesen, Ferhan Önder,

Myroslava Khomik, Shauna Li Roolvink, Tim Vogler, Michael Poll, Douglas Knehans, Elisabeth Plank, Dagmar Feyen, Chad Lawson, Matthew Patrick Morris, Edwin Cahill, Ann LIebeck, Bridget Casey, Robert Philips, Danielle Buonaiuto, Daniel Klein, André Callagaro, Brian Kauth, Nadia Preindl, Georgina Lester, Brigitte Ulbrich, Hanna Kristall, Cristina Prats Costa, Marianne Dumas, Josh Skorja, Sharon Carty, Eric Montalbetti, Antonio Piricone, Lydia Maria Bader, Gustavo Ubeda, Holly Mathieson, Kathrin Christians, Ferzan Önder, John Anderson, Lisa-Maria Jank, Hee Jun, Stephen Baron, Miriam Pascual, Elisabeth Krauss, B Terwey, Hoang Khang Pham, Holly Roadfeldt, Emi Ferguson, Jacqueline Kopacinski, Nicole Batchelar, Matthew Toogood, Christoph Urbanetz, Jamie Hall, Shie Rozow, Johannes Roetzer, Martin Owne, Hyung-ki Joo, Reinhard and Angelika Ernst, and many others. A sincere thank you!

Last but not least, we want to thank the person who patiently edited all of our text and worked tirelessly with us to make the book readable – our wonderful editor Youri Cho. We could not have wished for a better editor, who not only became a dear friend, but who also has the unique ability to edit our words in terms of flow, diction and personality. We cannot wait to do more with you, Youri!

Enjoy the book. We hope that it helps you in your career and gives us the opportunity to discover even more astonishing talents around the world.

Yours,

Bernhard Kerres   Bettina Mehne

Vienna, April 18, 2017

For Magdalena
B.K.

To my parents, who took me backstage right from the start
B.M.

Contents

[1]

CAREER STRATEGY

SIMPLY OPENING THIS BOOK is a big step - it means that you are thinking actively about your career, its development, and the business side of performing classical music. For many musicians, this is actually a very hard step. You love to make music and you love to perform. However, the business side of it all is probably very low on your priority list. Unfortunately, this is the exact part that ensures not only your survival, but also learning how to make a decent living overall.

In business, any new project or new business starts with a strategy. The term "strategy" comes from Greek, and means "the art of leading troops." It has its origins in military leadership and planning to achieve goals under conditions of high uncertainty. We recommend starting, or reassessing, your career with a strategy. The first step involves a self-coaching process, which we introduce below.

THE SELF-COACHING PROCESS

When coaching musicians, we like to use a process which begins by putting a bit of a distance between where you are today and where you would like to be. We'd like to take you through this process, and truly encourage you to actually write down the answers on a physical piece of paper for yourself. The mere act of writing helps get the blood flowing in the right direction. If you can't be bothered with a piece of paper, grab a pen and write your answers right into the margins of this book! The aim here is to help you develop a fresh perspective on your professional life.

Let's start by considering a short journey in time. Put yourself ten years ahead, i.e. into the year 2028. Now start describing the elements of your life in that year in detail:

- What will you be doing?

- What will you be working on?

- What excites you?

- What are you passionate about?

- How will you make money?

- With whom will you be working?

- Where will you be working?

- What does your private life look like?

- Are you traveling a lot or are you mostly staying in one place?

- What makes you happy?

Answer these questions honestly, and just for yourself. Describe the situation you see yourself in, in 2028, with as much detail as possible. Perhaps you want to share this with a third person, or simply just write it for yourself.

Now take a rest, and let it sink in. Then start the second step.

From this position of ten years ahead, e.g. 2028, look back over the last ten years. Consider the turning points of your career, the issues that really helped you, and the stumbling blocks.

- What was important over the last ten years that brought you to where you are?

- Who were the people who supported you? What did they do?

- Where did you get the best energy from?

- Where did you get the best advice from?

- Who influenced you most strongly?

- What did you do yourself that brought to where you are?

- Where did you stand in your own way?

Again, we highly recommend writing the answers to these questions down. Describe your path in as much specific detail as possible.

Writing these answers down helps you formulate the answers, clear your thought process, and most importantly, have documentation to look back at in the future.

Before you start with the third step, take another break and clear your head. Get some fresh air or you might even sleep on it. Then start again.

Start the third step by reading through your notes from steps one and two. Now formulate and write down your long-term goals as statements, e.g. "I am playing in a leading chamber ensemble with its own series of concerts in the US and recording contemporary music." Do not write down, "I want to...", as a goal should always be formulated as "I am...". Take care not to write more than three goals - often even one is enough. You might add another goal a year or so later. Now start writing down what you need to do *today* to get you to where you want to be in ten years time.

Break each goal down into actionable steps. To continue with our example: "I have found three congenial partners with whom I can form a quartet," or "We have commissioned six new pieces for a string quartet." Again, actionable steps are written down as achievements, not as something you merely wish to do. You need to be able to tick off concrete actions, as opposed to a wish list.

This forms the start of a career plan. You are well advised to discuss all your notes with colleagues, mentors and professors. Look for people who lift you up with positive energy, but are also realistic. Avoid people with neutral or negative energy. You are about to embark on a big journey. This will need a great deal of positive energy from you, but also from your surroundings.

This is not a one-time process, but an ongoing one and something we advise you to do every year, keeping track quarterly. Go back to your original notes and see what has changed. Reflect upon it and discuss it with your trusted circle. It is normal that things will evolve, you will change, and circumstances will vary. But a consistent career reflection process will help you to keep track of such changes and keep you focused on what is essential for you.

Herbert von Karajan once said that someone who achieves all their goals did not set them high enough. Keeping this in mind, it is important to assess whether your planned steps and goals are manageable, and analyze what might keep you from reaching them or determine if they are already slightly unrealistic to start with.

THE PORTFOLIO CAREER

Hopefully you did not graduate believing that your career would consist of solely playing in an orchestra or ensemble, or being a soloist. The truth is that times have changed significantly and you will most probably find yourself in a portfolio career.

The term portfolio career was first used by the business and management thinker, Charles Handy, in his book, "The Empty Raincoat" in 1994. With amazing foresight, he understood that the working world as we knew it then was changing quickly. Just as we are already seeing a dramatically shifting landscape in the business world due to technology developments, this changing environment is also a reality for music professionals. Rather than being scared, it actually offers significantly many more opportunities for the artist.

A portfolio career means that you can do several different jobs at the same time. As a classical musician, you might be a member of an orchestra, play chamber music regularly, perform as a soloist from time to time, and also teach. What used to be four different tracks can now be combined into a single career. There are a growing number of opportunities out there to add to your portfolio, making you a more varied artist, as well as a more competitive player on the world's stage. A recent blog post on the Future of Music lists 45 different revenue streams: money.futureofmusic.org/40-revenue-streams.

Violinist Alexej Igudesman is an outstanding soloist. Most of the time he performs with his friend pianist Hyung-ki Joo in their duo, Igudesman & Joo (www.hellostage.com/igudesmanandjoo). They develop their sketches and perform their programs all over the world, but Alexej also performs his own programs. Not only is he a great composer who writes works for the violin, but he has also written for Hollywood. In fact, he has an IMDb credit for the soundtrack of Sherlock Holmes.

Being a portfolio artist is actually already true for most composer/conductors, although the world sometimes only seems to see one dominant side of them. Composer Konstantia Gourzi (www.hellostage.com/Konstantia-Gourzi) is most often her own conductor when it comes to premiering her own work, like at the 2016 Summer Lucerne Festival, but she is also an avid supporter of the works of her composer colleagues. As a professor for contemporary music ensembles at the Academy for Music and Theatre in Munich, she has also created several ensembles within and outside the university, which are all thriving.

Performing in ensembles, orchestras and as a soloist may seem natural to you, as teaching may be as well. But as a musician in today's world, we would encourage you to look even beyond these worlds. Internet databases are always looking for music samples. Websites need sounds. Concerts in private places can generate much momentum. As the world continues to evolve, opportunities abound, and sometimes in unexpected places.

For example, check out Groupmuse (www.groupmuse.com). They've created an app where performers and music lovers can meet. Performers play in private homes, from tiny apartments to big mansions, for music lovers who gather together their own audience. The performers actually get paid directly by the audience. It's a wonderful and innovative model for bringing audiences and musicians together in an intimate atmosphere.

There are many things you can do yourself to expand your portfolio. The Austrian Auner Quartet (www.hellostage.com/aunerquartett), founded by the entrepreneurial violinist Daniel Auner (www.hellostage.com/danielauner), just started their second season of self-promoted concerts while this book was being written. Putting on yet another chamber music cycle in the city of music might seem like a crazy idea, but the Auner Quartet has been successful in doing so, and they are just one example. They were not shy in tackling the basics of promoting, marketing concerts, doing recordings, and learning how to manage other business aspects of their career. They delved into many details and taught themselves how to design posters and master recording tapes. All the quartet members also contacted their families and friends to market and sell their concert series. While the tasks may have proved daunting, this quartet was able to find a way to expand their career options.

London is another hub with many different concert series, but there still seems to be room for yet another one if you have the right idea. Cellist Julia Morneweg has gathered together a group of superb chamber musicians to bring a new concert series concept to London, and has added being a promoter to her portfolio (www.hellostage. com/profile/6708). To be able to present fresh and spontaneous programs, the actual content is only revealed to the audience at the concert, quite like the vegetable boxes you may order to arrive on your doorstep. This innovative concept has gained instant popularity in Hampstead and Battersea, and is quickly spreading throughout London.

A portfolio career will require playing or singing at your highest level, and only you and your artistic quality can be the motivating drive behind your career. However, artistic quality alone cannot enable a successful career – you have to actively manage your own career. This will require you to learn about management, the business, and how classical music works. It also requires time, effort and professionalism.

Just as you set time aside each day for practice, you will need to equally set time aside to manage your business affairs. This should not limit the quality of your practicing, but realistically, it will eat into your free time. However, it will be time well invested in learning to stay in contact with your network, follow up on opportunities, reply promptly, and stay on the ball.

The better you are at managing the business side of your career (without compromising your artistic quality), the easier it will be to work together with a manager in the future if you ever chose to do so. Not only will you then understand their work much better, you will also be able to appreciate what they are doing and better know how to support them best.

This book will help you understand many of the issues around your career and take more active steps in managing it. Continue to seek advice on the business side, take courses if you find good ones, look for coaches, and always maintain professionalism.

Your career, always, starts with you. Strategy goes hand in hand with knowing what makes you special. In the next chapter we will expand upon what a musician's brand is, and how branding and marketing set the foundations for finding and creating work.

[2]

PERSONAL BRAND

HAVE YOU EVER THOUGHT about how people actually see and perceive you? As an artist, you are out on stage, visible to hundreds, if not thousands of people. They follow you on social media. They become your fans. They engage you for performances. Who are you to them?

In this chapter, we will explore your personal brand – the side of you that is visible to colleagues, audiences, orchestras, and promoters. This side of you is not detached from you personally, but the professional world will not and should not see your complete private persona. Therefore it is important to think about your public persona, and how people may perceive, remember, and think of you.

We have already established the first important point: your public persona is not detached from your private one. Envision a Hindu temple. The doors are wide open and before you enter, you see a beautiful statue. To enter, you have to step across a threshold and then walk a zig-zag path to get into the inner sanctum of the temple. Your public persona probably goes as far as letting people get close to the statue, but not making it all the way into your private life. However, you will still want to think about how the gate, the threshold and the statue look, how people feel about it, and how they connect to it. This is you as a professional brand.

While we actually want to delve beyond brands and introduce the concept of Lovemarks, which was initially developed by Kevin Roberts, the former CEO of Saatchi & Saatchi, a worldwide marketing agency, we'll start with branding first.

What is a brand? A brand encompasses the projection of a specific image, lifestyle, or concept as applied to any business, person, or collective entity. Big brand names will come to mind quickly, such as Apple, Coca Cola, Google, Microsoft, Mercedes, and BMW, because they are known and trusted entities. Interbrand publishes an annual ranking of the best global brands (www.interbrand.com/best-brands/best-global-brands/2016/ranking/) and their methodology for the rankings is based upon three pillars of research:

- Financial analysis, looking at the economic profit

- Role of the brand as part of the purchase decision

- Brand strength in creating loyalty

As funny as it may sound, these same three categories are actually helpful when thinking of your own personal brand as a musician, artist, ensemble or institution as well.

> **Financial Analysis:** Making a living, and a good living, is an important, sometimes overlooked fact in classical music. In the end, you need to make money, and you will have certain needs and wishes that will require money. If you look at the biggest brands such as Apple and Google, they actually rarely speak about money. Rather, they are driven by their passion for their products and developments. However, it is this very passion that drives their financial success, and this success allows them to keep growing. Passion is a factor, but does not influence every decision. After all, finances will always

be a significant part of any equation, and making money will allow you to continue to grow and spread your vision.

Role of Brand: Have you ever thought about why promoters engage you or why audiences come to listen to you? Is it the program you play, the convenience of hearing another concert close by, or is it because they specifically want to hear *you*? Young artists have an advantage when performing in their own community, even if it is very small in the beginning, because everyone wants to hear them. They start out with a strong brand and strong support in a small market. The key is to grow to markets outside of the home market, working together with promoters, presenters and others, to add more markets beyond one's own territories.

Brand Strength: How often are you re-invited for concerts by the same promoter? How regularly do people come to your concerts? Would they come more than once a year? Creating loyalty amongst promoters and audiences is vital to your future success.

Some musicians implicitly work according to these principles, without ever having known anything about branding, or having had any awareness of such a concept. Others might have picked up on certain ideas or had someone coaching them.

Martin Grubinger (www.hellostage.com/martin-grubinger), the Austrian multi-percussionist, is a great example. Percussion was not really a solo instrument in classical music, with a notable few exceptions of great percussionists like Evelyn Glennie and Colin Currie. The repertoire was limited to music written by Iannis Xenakis, Bela Bartok and a few others.

But then a young blond country boy from Upper Austria came along with a big dream to move percussion from the back of the orchestra to the front, where solo instruments belonged, in his view. Martin Grubinger had played the drums since he was a small boy and was completely obsessed with it. He worked tirelessly day in and day out. He did not want to join an orchestra as just another percussionist, but rather, wanted to become a soloist. So this is what he worked on.

Today, Martin Grubinger is probably considered one of the biggest stars in classical music, and not just in percussion. Many great composers have written concertos for him, including Friedrich Cerha, Peter Eötvös, and Tan Dun. Rumors have it that John Williams wants to write a concerto for him. Martin Grubinger only plays contemporary music, which is always hard to sell anywhere in the world, yet his concerts are almost always completely sold out. How is that possible?

First of all, Martin Grubinger was able to leverage the role of his brand. People come to concerts directly because of him - not because of the repertoire, not because of the convenience of yet another concert, and not because of cheap tickets. Martin has been able to build a personal relationship with audiences around the world. Part of how he did this is his very likeable, no-stardom approach to his audiences. He often speaks at his concerts and introduces the music he is playing. He also formed a percussion group with some musician friends, called Percussive Planet, playing everything from classical music adaptations of popular music to film music, jazz, Latin American music, and even pop. His non-elitist approach always focuses on good music and playing better than everyone else, winning people's hearts in the process.

Martin's steady approach enabled him to quickly build loyalty among his followers. When he was the Artist in Residence in 2010/11 at the Wiener Konzerthaus in Vienna, his concerts during that season were not only of outstanding artistic quality and with an excellent program, but they were also completely sold out. Because of the artistic value, but also because of the sales success, a percussion subscription series was initiated at a leading concert venue – the first of its kind. The success of that subscription series at the Wiener Konzerthaus continues as we are writing this book.

Just as interestingly, Martin has been able to build a similar loyalty with promoters and orchestras around the world. He is always re-invited by conductors and promoters. They start planning their next projects right after his current concert has finished! With his passion and mission, Martin Grubinger creates excitement and enthusiasm in the people around him to work on the next project together.

Martin Grubinger's highly emotional connection to his audiences, but also to promoters, conductors and orchestras, is a great example for a true Lovemark, as Kevin Roberts[1] would define it. Roberts developed a simple but powerful matrix showing the difference between brands and Lovemarks.

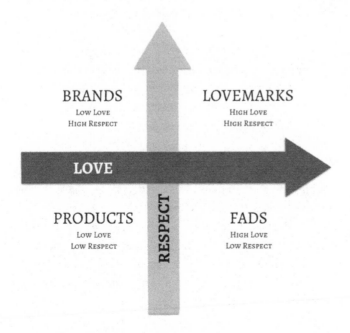

1 Kevin Roberts: Lovemarks: The Future Beyond Brands, 2005.

The matrix builds along two axes of love and respect. Both are very relevant to musicians and ensembles.

- **Respect:** The audience's respect for a classical musician increases accordingly by the musician's technical abilities and virtuosity.

- **Love:** The audience's love for a musician comes from the emotional connection which grows between the artist and the audience.

Let's take a look at the four quadrants and put them within context for classical musicians:

Products: Kevin Roberts describes products as utilities which are essential to our lives, but without any brand value. Think about your water utility or electricity. Often people do not even know the company name behind their utility supplier. Still, they are necessary and fulfill an important part in our daily lives. In the music world, we luckily have many reliable and good musicians who support the sound of an orchestra or a choir. They play an important role in our musical experience. However, they are part of a "Klangkörper", a body made up of many people producing a wonderful sound, rather than being the soloist in front.

Fads: These are the short term trends seen in the latest fashion idols, hairstyles, or gadgets. A have-to-have at that very moment, but without any long-term loyalty. In classical music we all have seen these short-term stars, the surprising winners of a competition, the YouTube stars, the ones playing one concerto better than anybody else. They are fascinating but they go just as fast as they come. Not a corner you necessarily want to be in if you want to have a long and successful career.

Brands: Kevin Roberts describes companies in this corner as having a lot of functional benefits, and always being brighter, stronger, and better, but with a low emotional connection. You will find musicians like this too. These are the fantastic musicians with great virtuosity and amazing technique, but somehow they do not touch your soul. Sometimes this may be subject to daily variations, or sometimes to the subjective impression that audience members might get.

Lovemarks: Kevin Roberts explains that only customers – in our case, audiences – get to decide which brands actually fall into this quadrant. It is all about the deep emotional connection. We are sure that each of our readers would be able to immediately name musicians belonging in this corner, and we are lucky to have so many in the classical music world.

So the magic question becomes, how does one actually get into the Lovemarks quadrant as a musician? We will not delve into the artistic quality, technical capabilities, and virtuosity that one needs to get into this quadrant. Rather, let's explore what love means in this context.

Kevin Roberts writes about the ingredients of love: mystery, sensuality, and intimacy. Doesn't music fall exactly within this realm? How can you use these ingredients to develop and grow your own Lovemark?

Mystery is all about telling stories, but its most critical component is based on the things that we leave out, or just hint at. Translated from ancient Greek, *mysterium* means secret, and is often associated with a hidden religious truth. However, music, too can serve as a conduit to truth, shrouded in mystery. Some musicians see themselves as a vessel of great music written by composers, bringing to life the mysteries of their musical thoughts and ideas. Considering and enjoying this mystery of music might be a start for many musicians.

Sensuality involves all our five senses. Even though, as musicians, we are often mostly concerned about what people hear, we should not neglect the other senses. Obviously, how we look on stage makes a big difference. Sensuality does not call for short dresses and a sexy appearance, but rather, it is about your energy. Your appearance in the level of comfort you feel can be sensed positively by an audience member. This energy is often felt in how musicians enter a stage, not only for performances, but also for rehearsals, which makes a huge difference. The Kronos Quartet was probably the first classical music ensemble to stage their appearances on concert stages to make themselves as visually fascinating as their music itself. Smell is an often underrated but actually most critical sense. One might be surprised by how many department stores, but also museums, actively stimulate this sense in their visitors. The Abercrombie & Fitch stores around the world might be the most obvious example, but many others work significantly subtler. For many soloists and conductors, this is naturally a big challenge because of the setting of the venue, working hard on a stage in bright light. As a concert hall however, one might want to glean knowledge from museums and other cultural institutions, such as their use of florals or the smell of the programs. Touch is a sense that audiences will mostly see in the artist's handling of their instrument. Just think of the difference amongst pianists, with some using almost brute force hammering into the keyboard while others using the softest touch imaginable.

Taste is an interesting sense in the context of music. If you think of going to a great restaurant with friends or spending an evening home relaxing while cooking, inevitably there is music playing in the background. These senses are more intermingled than many people realize, and sometimes music can trigger or heighten this sense immeasurably. It can also be as simple as enjoying a glass of wine at a concert, or for the artists, enjoying a fresh beer coming off stage after a great performance! When we were working at the Wiener

Konzerthaus, we often had such refreshments ready right offstage for the artists, which was always very much appreciated.

Music itself is probably one of the most intimate forms of communication between people on a very sensual level. Intimacy connotes empathy, passion and commitment. It is amazing how some of the greatest artists can create an intimate setting with a solo recital in a hall with several thousand seats. They share their passion with their audience and engage them in an empathic, highly emotional dialogue. Intimacy is about opening up to this dialogue between the musicians on stage and the audience members, creating those unique moments that all of us have experienced at one point or another.

With all these words about branding and Lovemarks, about sharing emotions with audiences and fellow musicians, about making music passionately and much more, ultimately it all boils down to you. Everything we have written about needs to feel natural to you and this will probably change over time. A "Lovemark" should never be a forced part of your public persona, but rather, discovered, as you figure out what is important to you and what you want to express with your music.

See for yourself how you perceive some of the biggest stars in classical music. Try to see musicians like Grigory Sokolov, Hillary Hahn, Wynton Marsalis, Gabriela Montero and many others live. Ask yourself which quadrant you would put them in and why. Discuss it with fellow musicians, non-musical friends, and audience members. This will help you to find your very own Lovemark identity over time naturally, not by copying, but by going through an ongoing reflection process. Remember that most of these artists did not make a deliberate and conscious decision about what makes their brand unique, but rather followed their own callings and instincts. Grigory Sokolov simply feels more comfortable when the hall is dark, Patricia

Kopatchinskaja feels more connected to the stage when performing barefoot, and Hélène Grimaud loved wolves. Your own Lovemark is probably already there and only needs to be discovered by yourself.

[3]

MARKETING

ARTISTS OFTEN FEEL UNCOMFORTABLE when confronted with business terminology such as marketing and sales. They can become especially uncomfortable at the notion that they themselves could be the product that needs to be marketed or sold, and artists can often feel that their artistry has little value in today's world. Well, this is all perfectly understandable.

However, let's try another spin on these terms. Think of marketing as a conversation you enter into with people who are interested in classical music and in what you are doing in particular. Sales can be thought of as giving these people the opportunity to actually experience your musicianship and art.

Before we delve into marketing, let's look into the difference between marketing and branding. Simply put, branding is all about how you are seen by people, whereas marketing is all about making them see you. Branding is about the image others have about you. Marketing encompasses the communication tools used to bring that image to the world.

That being said, we will expand upon marketing and sales as general business terms in order to help you better understand how you can use these practices to further your career.

INTRODUCTION TO MARKETING

When we define marketing as a conversation between people, we also need to keep in mind that there should be a purpose to this conversation. The purpose should focus on an exchange of interests, and on the information you have for your fellow conversationalists. This information will – not exclusively, but often – contain information about the sales of your products and services. That can include upcoming concerts, masterclasses you may give, teaching availabilities, etc.

Edmund Jerome McCarthy, a marketing professor at Michigan State University, the University of Oregon and the University of Notre Dame introduced the concept of the Four P's. The Four P's stand for:

- Product

- Price

- Place, and

- Promotion

The product is you. It describes what you are doing, such as you are a violinist, but it goes much further than that. Your product descriptions will need to get across what makes you special and unique, and create the "box" in which people can place you. It is an easy and clear summary of your personal brand. People need to understand the product first, i.e. a fizzy drink, before they can then associate it with a brand, i.e. Coca-Cola. For a musician, they will first need to understand what instrument you play or what voice you sing, before learning about what makes you special.

Price is what you charge for your services, and pricing will always depend on various market forces, with the simplest being supply and demand. But these two basic factors can become magnified by issues such as timing, repertoire, etc. For example, you will always get paid a little more if you are jumping in at the last minute saving a production or concert than you would under normal circumstances. An unspoken rule exists that when you jump in, you will receive something between your standard fee with the promoter and what the person you are filling in for would have received. It obviously depends on who you are replacing; if you are still at a beginner level and you happen to take over for a high fee superstar, you cannot expect anything near their fee, but somewhere higher than what a promoter would normally pay for someone starting out. Situations such as these can sometimes work out beautifully if you can get a re-invitation and retain the negotiated fee as your entry level with this particular promoter.

We have a whole chapter devoted to negotiations (see NEGOTIATING YOUR FEE), but for now, it is important just to understand the supply and demand for everything you do. If you are the only violin teacher in a city where all the parents want their children to learn violin, you can charge much higher prices than if you are one of hundreds of harp teachers in a town where no one wants to learn that instrument. Make sure you understand the dynamics for everything you do and that you research what others charge for similar services. These are always good benchmarks.

Place is all about where your "product" is available. You should think about your home market first – the place you live and spend most of your time in, then the country you are in, and then the continent. For artists based in Europe, it is already difficult to perform in

North America. Not only are visa regulations a concern, but the travel costs associated with going to a different continent are often too high for a promoter on another continent to engage you, unless your government or someone else will pay for the intercontinental travel cost. But in today's world, sense of place is changing with the internet. It is important to think about where and how your products can be made available through the internet. For example, music downloads and streaming is one area. Teaching over the internet is also becoming more popular. We think that the internet will offer many more opportunities for musicians to market and sell their products and services in the future.

Promotion is what many people often mistake as marketing. However, it is only one aspect of marketing. Promotion entails making information about the product, the place, and the price available. Musicians sometimes think that promotion is the work of agents, PR agencies, managers or the promoters. Though partly true, promotion has become more and more an important part of a musician's work. Promotion can happen through various channels, from printed material to CDs, to your online presence and social media. We will discuss several channels here as well as in separate dedicated chapters.

Beyond the Four P's, there are a couple more concepts that are relevant for musicians. You might have heard the terms B2B (Business to Business) and B2C (Business to Consumer). Well, as great as these terms are, life for musicians is a bit more complex unfortunately. Yes, the first B is always you. But more often than not, you then sell your product through managers, promoters, orchestras, ticket sales organizations (all B's) to your audience (the C). You therefore have to consider both models of B2B as well as B2C.

Your B2B marketing focuses on connecting with promoters, presenters, orchestras, etc. who will eventually hire you. These people are often flooded with information. Getting through that "noise" is not necessarily easy. Having relevant information available for these B's to look up easily and keeping them regularly informed without annoying them is an art in itself. The good news is that in today's age, various opportunities exist, especially in the digital space, which is why you will find a whole chapter in this book dedicated to your digital presence.

Nevertheless, thinking about B2C is equally important. A starting point is your own fan base. Again, there is a whole chapter in this book about your fan base. But it is good to think broader, such as thinking about the audiences of venues you are playing in, people interested in your instrument, your favorite composers, etc. Entering into a conversation with the C's will help you increase your fan base. Social media is one great tool for that. But you would be surprised to find that societies and associations for a wide variety of classical music from instruments to certain composers around the world exist. Getting to know them and building a relationship to the relevant ones can help. Part of your B2C communication is also classical PR (public relations). PR in today's world not only includes newspapers, radio stations and TV, but blogs such as Bachtrack (www.bachtrack. com) which has gained a wide following amongst classical music fans.

Another important concept to understand is push versus pull marketing. The name itself already gives the concepts away. Push marketing entails any kind of marketing activity where you actively send information out or do proactive promotions. On the other hand, pull marketing compels people out there in the world to seek available information, without requiring your active assistance to make it happen in that moment. A good push marketing campaign will inspire people to pull more information about you.

Push marketing can be broadly addressed, e.g. to your followers on social media or recipients of your newsletter. However, better push marketing is specifically targeted to a small group of people for whom the message is actually relevant. You will not write to your fans that you have just studied a new role and are happy to perform it soon. This is information that is much more relevant to a selected number of opera houses and conductors. When target marketing, it is important to not to overload people with push marketing activities. This means keeping information short and relevant, and enabling them to find more in other places if they are interested. It also means pacing your push marketing carefully across various channels. While it is common in some social media channels to send information even multiple times in a day, sending out a daily newsletter would be a nuisance to your recipients and would probably backfire quickly.

Pull marketing is often treated secondarily, but has gained significant importance in classical music and the professional service space. For you, it means keeping relevant information easily available and accessible where people can find it quickly. You would be surprised by how many artists' bios are floating around in print and online, mostly outdated, or by how few artists keep their upcoming concerts updated on relevant platforms and their website up-to-date. Keep in mind that Facebook or LinkedIn are not relevant platforms for making information accessible and available. These are push-channels, not pull-channels. You should start by making a (short) list of information that is relevant for B's and for C's to find out about you, then post each item where people can find it. This should include your personal website if you have one, your HELLO STAGE page, and information a manager might have on file for you. Make it a habit to dig out the list at least once a month, look at what you need to revise where, and update it across all places.

Market segmentation is another important concept to understand. This term merely means grouping all your possible customers into various categories according to similar behaviors and needs. These groups are called segments.

We actually already did segmentation just a few paragraphs up – segmenting your potential market between professionals and audiences, as you would market very differently to each of these groups. Considering further segmentation is always sensible, but to start, general segmentation that can be useful can be broken down by:

- **Geography:** Knowing which countries people work and live in is important. This avoids sending information about your upcoming US tour to promoters in Indonesia.

- **Contact level:** There is a difference between someone you are close friends with and someone you were just introduced to via email. Our category recommendations would be:

  - Close friends

  - Friends

  - Acquaintances

  - Others

- **Organization Level:** For professional contacts, three to four levels should be fine, addressing the range from decision-makers to support staff.

- **Category:** Is it an orchestra, a concert hall promoting by itself, a promoter without a hall, a conductor, a singer, musician...

This segment information should form part of your contact database. This enables you to quickly reach out to opera houses in Spain if you happen to be there and would like to arrange for an audition, or you can let conductors in Japan know that you have just successfully played a specific concert by a Japanese composer.

A good segmentation strategy combined with an easy-to-use database enables you to achieve highly effective marketing, instead of just spamming people. It is one of the most powerful concepts and tools in marketing.

The last general concept we would like to introduce here is the concept of touch points. Touch points are moments where and when consumers – your audience, but also promoters and others - come in contact with you, your product, and your art. You would be surprised by the sheer amount of touch points others may have with you, from your website, to your recordings, concerts, performances, meetings, etc. The magic lies in staying consistent to your personal brand whenever people may have contact with you.

A wonderful example in this respect is the Austrian mezzo soprano Maria Weiss (www.hellostage.com/maria-weiss). Maria focuses on early music and enjoys contemporary music. She has a very bright, clear voice, and is one of the most beautiful ones you could probably find for early music. Her hobbies include baking, cooking and photography. If you look at her social media accounts, you will find many bright, mostly white photos, beautifully arranged with flowers and food. Her first solo album, "Favola in Musica" not only contains the most beautiful music, but is made with a unique personal style. Whenever you get in touch with Maria anywhere, you feel her unique personality shine through, and can sense a perception of her on stage. It is an amazing application of the touch point concept, although she probably does it just because this is who she is, not necessarily thinking of marketing or branding.

The other "secret" of touch points is that your consumers will need to have been in touch at least seven times before they will enter into any kind of conversation. This is also pretty true for the business world. Unless a promoter has heard about you consistently several times, you likely will not be engaged. Marketing and getting one's name out there takes time and patience. After developing the concept and the message, you should not change it, but stay with it - even if you feel it is already so boring and you have evolved so much. The reality is that it takes significantly longer for your network and the people you want to be interested in you to actually receive and process the message. Therefore stay on the message, and be consistent and persistent.

After this general introduction, we will discuss how marketing can actually be done and what the various tools are. An important lesson is also that marketing is actually done personally a lot more than you might think. You will always the best billboard for yourself. Later we will address several other tools.

YOU FOR YOURSELF

No fancy tools, no big secrets, no great expertise – just you. Marketing and sales starts with you. And only you. Every time you meet someone, every time you drop a line to someone, every time you are performing, you are always marketing yourself, even if you are not aware of it. So now is a good time to start thinking about all of this!

Your most powerful marketing and sales tool is your own, personal network. We focus here on your professional network, but another whole chapter is dedicated to your fan base, your end-consumer network.

Your personal network starts early. These contacts will include the first colleagues you study with, the teachers you learn from, and the masterclasses you attend (pay attention to the guys organizing the masterclass – they may go on to have other jobs in the classical music industry and you want them to remember you, i.e. hire you). Every encounter with someone related to the professional side of classical music is an opportunity to grow and strengthen your network. Doing this is so easy that it is surprising to see how few musicians do it.

Your peers are more important than you think. Among your peers are conductors who might one day be looking for exactly what you have to offer. There are composers who are glad if you perform their works. There are other instrumentalists wanting to form an ensemble. There are often colleagues who switch sides from actively making music to management and administration. They just might remember you and think of you in the right moment. Being a valuable part of your peer network is important. This means that you have to give in order to receive. It is often the small things that count, such as going to concerts or exams of colleagues, helping them out on a difficult assignment, or jumping in when they need someone. Whatever seeds you plant in your network will eventually bear fruit at some point, but most importantly, you will be rewarded by the great joy of working with and supporting your peers.

Many great artists also make a point of supporting young artists. Take for instance, the Järvi family of great conductors who initiated the Pärnu Music Festival and Järvi Academy (www.parnumusicfestival.ee), bringing together young musicians and conductors who happen to be the most fantastic soloists around with their family friends. Every summer they work together for two weeks in Estonia. Like the Jarvi family, many well-known conductors and soloists are very approachable and take great interest in the next generation of musicians. Do not be shy in going backstage to the Green Room after a concert and introducing yourself! Again, you cannot expect to get an engagement out of one visit to the Green Room after a concert, or even an audition. But you would be surprised by how many great artists register who come by after a concert. At some point, you might ask if you could just play for them.

Going to concerts and visiting the Green Room afterwards is not just about getting an audition or gig for yourself. First of all, listening to live music is one of the greatest and most important experiences you can have. But more importantly, you will also find yourself together with other musicians. They will have tips for you. You can learn from them. You might even make music with them some day. Therefore – go to concerts and congratulate the artists afterwards!

COMPETITIONS

One big question in marketing yourself is the role of competitions. There are many opinions floating around about the value and the fairness of them. Should you bother? A competition gives you the opportunity to perform - under immense stress and often in front of people you would not normally play or sing for. Some competitions, however, do draw a huge public following through broadcasting and live streaming.

We would argue that competitions are a good opportunity, even if they are not perfect circumstances. They can often provide the chance to play in front of important people who might be able to help you onto your next step, even if you are not among the finalists. Asking them for their opinion and advice might give you totally new insights. Listening to your colleagues can also give you a feeling of where you are yourself, and help you see your own level more objectively.

Of course, it goes without saying that you should choose which competitions to participate in wisely. Starting with the biggest competitions for your instrument might not be the way to go. Start with smaller competitions with good professors or artists in the jury. Learn about playing competitions and how to best cope with them, then work your way up. Just a little side tip: if you get as far as the round playing with/conducting an orchestra, please don't list them in your biography as one of the Orchestras you have performed with – it only shows that you wanted to disguise the fact that it was in a competition only and tried to pass it off as a proper engagement, which does not look good.

MARKETING TOOLS

The digital world brings us more and more marketing tools each and every day. Using them has become much easier than ever before, and offers great opportunities for individuals, ensembles and others who thus far could not afford any big campaigns. However, it can also lead to an information overflow, so using them wisely is important.

When thinking about marketing, most people immediately think of advertising. Although advertising is just one of many tools out of the marketing box, it is worth discussing briefly. Advertising can be interesting for musicians and ensembles. Often it is very specific to the local culture, but can quickly become very expensive and ineffective. It is good to look around at what other musicians and ensembles are doing. In some cultures, it is very normal to have musicians announce their concerts in newspapers. In other cities, promoters use billboards. Yet then again, there are places where artists should not do any real advertising themselves.

Before starting any advertising, you should first think of your goal. What do you want to achieve with advertising? What is your budget? Who is your market? Only then does it make sense to think about utilizing it.

One of the best advertising tools today is actually offered by social media platforms, especially, currently, by Facebook. Facebook allows you to target your advertising according to a long list of useful parameters, so that you can ensure it really reaches the people you want to target. With a few dollars, you can generate great relevant success. However, there is also a caveat. Once you start spending money with Facebook, they would obviously like for you to continue to do so. Although not proven, it seems that Facebook Pages that stop spending money suddenly get significantly less traffic than before, so just a note to be aware.

Public Relations (PR) is another important marketing tool. PR is your connection to the press and media, and is mostly country specific. Good PR requires good contacts with journalists, publications and media outlets. In every country you will find very good PR agencies focused on classical music. They have the relevant contact network and can support your activities. Keep in mind though that engaging a PR agency only makes sense when you are at a more advanced stage. You will need regular performances in that country and upcoming news such as an album release or an upcoming appointment, etc. Of course, exceptions to this general rule apply as well. If you have a great story or a project coming up in which you are truly driving yourself, a PR agency might be just what you need to give it that extra push; for example, if you are setting up your own mini-concert series or such, it could make sense. But make sure that the agency takes into consideration that you are only starting out and that they reflect that in their fee. We see a general shift in artists looking for PR early on in their career, rather than looking for management. Getting your name out and known for a project you did can be super helpful in attracting management. Hence we see a growing number of publicists and agencies who offer PR to young artists.

Some PR agencies will tell you that they can cover more than one country or more areas in North America. It is always sound to check this claim and speak with other clients to see if the agency truly can deliver that. When engaging a PR agency, agree on a plan, on desired results, and a corresponding budget. Then check in every several months, knowing that you will not see any real results in the first three months.

One of the best tools we have today is an electronic newsletter. We go in further detail on fan newsletters in the FANS chapter. But know that you can generate one for your professional network, one that addresses promoters, presenters, orchestras, etc.

A newsletter to your professional network should only go out a few times a year, understanding that most arts organizations are already overwhelmed with emails and work. Keeping them concise and relevant to the news they really need is essential. A major award, a new appointment, or an album release creates relevance and justifies a newsletter. Other than that, the professional community will always know where to find you, as long as you keep your instruments of pull marketing available.

[4]

BIOGRAPHY

ONE OF YOUR MOST important tools in marketing is your own biography. Artists' biographies are a special pet subject. Though we have seen so many and there are always interesting and special people behind them, rarely are they an interesting read! The whole process is always an ongoing discussion between artists, managers and promoters, but unfortunately people tend to hang onto bad examples and keep copying the same mistakes over and over again.

Let's look at the average structure of many biographies:

"XYZ started playing the piano at the age of four and went on to study with ABC and won the competition in Small-town at the age of 10..." - Anyone in advertising will tell you that you have way less than a minute to catch people's attention or you will otherwise lose their interest, so please skip birth and childhood, unless you are currently a child prodigy. The paragraph normally goes on to mention another few competitions the musician has ever gotten recognized for. Since it is a myth anyway that winning a competition will make your career, it is best to skip these altogether and not mention them unless you actually won any prizes at one of the major competitions not too long ago. Of course we are not saying that you shouldn't take part in these

competitions, as there are a whole lot of different things to be gained from doing so. What we are highlighting is that listing a bunch of competitions, though it may seem to lend legitimacy, does not help keep your reader's attention.

Next in the biography is mostly a lengthy list of orchestras and venues where the artist has played as a soloist/conductor or performed at in recital/chamber music. These lists are terrible to read, and instead of showing the level of with whom or where the artist has performed at, it actually makes the reader skip this section or just lose interest altogether. An equally long discography does exactly the same.

We finally find relevant information about what the artist is currently up to, as well as any future plans in the 3rd and 4th paragraphs, which has now unfortunately been buried underneath a lengthy lists of names of orchestras, collaborators and venues.

In cases where the artist is a string player, the biography might conclude with some information about the valuable instrument they are playing.

Of course we certainly agree that all of the above is very relevant information and needs to be shared with a) potential promoters, and b) your audience and fans. But not all of this information is relevant all the time, so you therefore need more than one version of your bio on hand:

- the long version, written for people in the music business you would like to impress, deal with, and create lasting relationships with;

- a shorter version that would mostly be used for program books and would contain relevant information for your audience;

- a short paragraph to serve as a quick and snappy introduction.

Though your long bio is best kept to no more than 750 words, it really should be around 500 words to be honest. The shorter, the better, as more people will read it. It's your bio, not an entire autobiography.

As a general rule of thumb, your short bio is just your long bio stripped of a lot of the history, and focusing heavily on your current and upcoming projects like recently-released CDs, collaborations, etc. You will also want to add a bit of personal information to this one. Audiences always love to find out a little bit more than just what you are up to professionally. For example, *"XY lives in New York City with his family and 3 dogs,"* or *"In her free time, YZ enjoys sailing her boat on Lake Geneva."* Anything that does not give away too much info, but that people can relate to, is good.

Often in program books, there is not enough room for even a short bio, especially in cases where there is more than one soloist in the concert. To avoid someone shortening your bio for you and thereby potentially missing the parts that are most important for you, you should have an introductory paragraph to supply them as well. This is probably the hardest to compose, but you will find that it has many uses and will not only be used for the purpose above.

In some countries, a more CV style bio is required for auditions, competitions or master classes, especially if you are a singer. Start a CV on your computer (Apple Numbers or Microsoft Excel are great software for this!), giving basic information in bullet points in chronological order, listing concerts and education. Once you have this saved, it is easy to add your latest news as you go along and you will always have it on hand when needed. But please don't send this spreadsheet to promoters and orchestras, as they won't be happy with it. They are looking for a biography written in full sentences.

Let's go back to the contents of your biography and how to best write one so that it captures your audience's attention.

1ST PARAGRAPH:

Start with an introductory sentence that clearly defines the essentials: your instrument (in case it is not mentioned next to your name already), where you are from, and perhaps a positive quote about your music from a known figure in the industry you have worked with or perhaps from a review:

"Norwegian pianist XYZ is best known for his Chopin interpretation, as the New York Times writes: ...."

2ND PARAGRAPH:

Here you should address what is currently happening with you: a position you might be holding, your engagements for this season, a new CD or digital release that is coming up.

In case you have a busy season, don't list everything, but only mention the highlights! It's always good to mention re-invitations, as they show potential new contacts that you have been liked at the places you have performed at and that they are keen to have you back.

3RD AND 4TH PARAGRAPHS:

At this point, you can talk about past seasons, as well as background information about your studies and major prizes you have won. In case you incorporated re-invitations in the above paragraph, don't mention these same institutions again, but maybe conductors or soloists you have worked with instead. Of course, you are proud of each single engagement, but you should only pick a few. If you are still at the beginning of your career, please resist listing the orchestras you have met in competitions amongst the ones you have actually performed with in concert. Something like this is easily spotted and does not go down well – unless they engaged you for a concert, they don't belong in this list. If you choose to do so, you can mention orchestras in context of the competition you took part in, but please note that this should be separate than ones you have performed with.

ENDING:

As a string player, here is where you should include information about your instrument. If it was given to you by an institution, this should definitely be mentioned as well. In fact, you will often have been committed to doing so and will need to keep an eye on this info not being erased by the promoter. There might also be a good story behind how you got your instrument, even if it is not by a famous maker. This would also be something of note with regard to the personal touch we discussed above.

The ending is also a good place for a quote about you in case you decided against opening your bio with one. Also, if you enjoy teaching or hold a position as a professor somewhere, this is the place to mention this.

FOOTNOTE:

You should put the date you last updated your biography underneath it. This is vital and often forgotten!

A promoter might put your bio aside and pull it out again if something triggers them to suddenly remember you. If they are not familiar with your latest whereabouts, they might mistake an outdated biography for the current one and consequently miss out on your latest developments. Most of the time, situations like this will cause you to miss out on an opportunity.

But also in their haste, program book editors often surf the net and grab the bio they can find easiest, which could easily be out of date. By putting a date or the season it is valid for at the bottom of your bio, they will know they have found the current one.

Make it a regular part of your plan to update all your bios often to keep them dynamic and always up-to-date. If you experience a big milestone, such as landing an important concert, booking a tour, signing with a label or celebrating any other major success, revise your bio immediately. Regardless, you should be revisiting your bio at least every 2-3 months, even if nothing has happened that was not mentioned before. Concerts that already took place should be mentioned in the past tense as the season progresses. A well-crafted bio is a forward-looking document that reflects where you are now and your plans for the immediate future.

It is advisable to have your biography in English as well as in your mother tongue or the language of the places where you often perform. Any promoter will appreciate not having to translate it, and the bonus effect is that you will have it exactly as you intended, rather than someone making a mess of translating it (a task often given to the young people in an office without the relevant experience of knowing the ins and out yet).

When determining where to use each bio for your website, HELLO STAGE, social media pages, and in your press and promotional materials, keep in mind that people have very short attention spans in general. But do include both your short and long bios on your official website.

For your HELLO STAGE page, you will need the short paragraph you created for your About section, and choose your short biography for the Biography section. The short paragraph will also be good for your Facebook, Twitter, etc. Your long biography should be included

in mailings to potential promoters. Once you have landed an engagement, don't forget to send them the short version nearer to the time
of the concert, so that the right one goes into the program book.

[5]

PHOTOS AND VIDEOS

YOUR BIOGRAPHY IS ONE part of your marketing material. A vital addition to any marketing package encompasses your photos and videos.

A photo is probably the first thing your audience will notice about you, and we are counting promoters, opera companies and orchestras in this category as well. After all, we all like to associate a name with a face, and your photo, whether it is on your website, HELLO STAGE Page, on a CD, poster or in a program book, is what everyone will see before they have even heard you play or sing a single note. This photo is the image they will have of you, and let's face it - it will even influence the way they are going to hear you.

When undergoing the process of having new publicity shots taken, you should ask yourself the following questions and discuss a few things with the photographer of your choice:

- What is the message you want to capture in your photograph? What image do you want to create for yourself and your music?

Be authentic! Don't try to do something that is not you, just because it seems to be the latest trend. In other words, don't focus on what everybody else is doing.

Don't include photos just because "they look good"; you want to show your individual personality and visually express what you are about. Recap what you have read in the Chapter PERSONAL BRAND and take your notes to discuss them with the photographer.

Focus on what makes you unique, and communicate this - with your face, how you position yourself, with what you wear, and if you don't happen to be a singer or a conductor, your instrument. Please resist a baton photo if you are a conductor unless you have a compelling idea as to how to position it; having scores with you looks way better for example. Together with the photographer, you want to ensure that the details express what you want your audience to understand about you.

It is good to keep in mind that there is no universal taste in photos all over the world; sometimes you will find that what works well in Germany is not such a great hit in France, the US or Asia. This should not stop you from creating your photo. When you start getting stronger in a market that might require a different approach, you can tailor make something for that market specifically.

However, here are a few practical tips as well:

Ask the photographer to make sure the photo "works" in color as well as in black & white, as you may not know what your promoter might prefer. Often they will need it in color for brochures and posters, but your photo will end up in b/w in the program book. If you only supply it in b/w, it might not be included in other material, or will look very odd next to color photos your colleagues have supplied.

You should have photos available in various formats too. There should be shots in landscape orientation, portrait and square. The more photos you supply promoters and marketers with that they can use, the less they will start cropping photos and sometimes distorting them.

When reviewing photos, also consider what they may look like when cut down to just your face. Very often there is only limited space next to your biography in a program book, and rather than printing the whole photo, it will most likely be reduced to stamp size showing only your head, so that the audience can still fairly recognize you.

Another word of advice for the ladies amongst you: make sure you also have a photo with something covering your shoulders, in case you decide to wear something strapless. This way you can avoid looking naked in a cropped photo.

Photos should be stored in high resolution in an online folder easily accessible for downloads. Dropbox is a good solution for this. You can then simply send people the link to your folder when they need your photographs. Make sure that all photos always include copyright information. At the least, the copyright should include information on which photos can be used free of charge, as well as the name of the photographer and your name. Make sure that this copyright information is agreed upon with each photographer. The custom is that you should provide photos for the marketing and publicity of your performances and work as a musician free of charge. If these photos are used for other purposes, e.g. in advertising for products, an ad campaign for an orchestra or other such activities, make sure that you have checked this with the photographer. He may be entitled to a fee for extended copyright usage. Also, always save photo files using your full name as the file name to ensure that your name is spelled correctly when people use said photos.

Promoters generally prefer to watch a video over being sent a sound file or a CD. Therefore, it is important for you to control what they may see when they look you up online, or what you may send them proactively. It used to be customary that singers especially would travel to audition at opera houses. Although that still happens, they are now all pre-selected via videos that have been sent in, so presenting you in the best possible way is key in getting the chance to meet decision makers in the flesh.

The thought process that went into your photoshoot likewise applies to filming a video. However, the most critical difference here should also be the key focus – sound! You have to make sure that the sound recorded is of the highest standard possible. The quality of the visual aspect does not matter in quite the same way and does not necessarily need to be state of the art, as long as the way you present yourself reflects what you are about. Focusing only on the visual element rather than paying attention to the sound will result in people switching your video off.

It is advisable to find a place to film with good acoustics rather than videotaping a performance somewhere, unless the venue happens to be equipped for that purpose. When you happen to be at the beginning of your career, you can probably ask your university if they are able to lend you the necessary equipment, but these days, one can even combine a smartphone camera with a decent mic to get a fairly good result.

As for the repertoire, pick something that you are really comfortable with and one that reflects what you are about musically. Try and film several shorter pieces or movements, rather than a whole sonata or concerto. This way the viewers of your video have a choice and will get a chance to learn more about you. It is advisable to not only record solo pieces, but also have a pianist accompany you.

If you are a conductor, the situation is slightly different, of course. It is hard to organize a studio situation for you, as hiring a whole orchestra is cost intensive. Orchestra managers will also be keen to see you rehearse, which is way more telling for them than a performance. Try and negotiate with the orchestras you rehearse with, to see if you can film yourself, then look for interesting passages you can send out. Don't be surprised if you hit a brick wall, since it is quite a tricky thing to get an orchestra's permission, but it is certainly worth a try.

When using videos to introduce yourself to promoters, make sure that they can actually see you. They are less interested in the cinematic artistry of the videographer than seeing you in action. They want to see your fingers moving on the piano, and they want to see how you stand and move on stage while performing. They are not interested in long shots or beautiful landscapes with your voice singing in the background.

When producing such videos, try to create several short videos with different kinds of music, such as a fast and virtuoso piece, or a quiet and romantic one. Show them the breadth and depth of your artistry, but do keep the videos short. Our viewing habits are driven by social media where Instagram videos are less than a minute, and a promoter will lose interest if there is a three-minute intro before you even start playing.

Store these different videos online where promoters can also find other information about you. We recommend using sites like HELLO STAGE so that your videos, bio and repertoire are all in one place and makes it easy for a promoter to get to know you.

When shooting a promotion video for an album, other rules apply. These promotion videos are aimed at the general public to drum up interest in your album. These videos can be much more artistic, but as always, should showcase your personality and style.

[6]

DIGITAL PRESENCE

ONCE UPON A TIME you would not have been found as a musician, ensemble or singer unless your management had listed you in one of those thick books with all the names and contact details of the Who's Who in classical music. Luckily those days are long gone and the internet now offers a multitude of opportunities for classical musicians to represent themselves online, exactly as they wish.

In this chapter we will cover your digital presence. While we will devote a different chapter to social media, this chapter is very much focused on information found about you on the internet.

The great opportunity that an online presence provides also comes with the challenge of keeping your digital profiles updated and relevant. People will no longer ask you to send your repertoire list and latest bio. Instead, they will just get it from your HELLO STAGE page or your own webpage. If your latest concerto or opera role is not listed on there and it was perhaps just what a promoter was looking for, there is no way for you to even know that you missed an opportunity.

Another great challenge is ensuring that your digital presence can actually be found. No one will Google "Pianist for Beethoven's 5th Piano Concerto". If they do, they will find millions of entries, including among them many fantastic, but now deceased pianists. In the good old days, no one put "pianist" besides their name in the general phonebook hoping someone would find them that way and engage them. You had to be in the pianist section of one of the specialist directories of musicians. These printed directories are clearly going out of business, therefore you want to ensure you are in the online directories for classical musicians, e.g. HELLO STAGE.

Having a digital presence in today's world is not only a necessity, but offers musicians the opportunity to present themselves much more broadly than ever before. If you go back only a few decades, musicians were very limited in presenting themselves. They might have had a printed business card and a folder. If they were lucky, they had a recording, but even that was difficult to send out and to take around before CDs arrived. Today a musician establishes visibility, credibility, and professionalism with a clearly thought through, up-to-date digital presence. It is therefore vital to utilize this for the benefit of your career. This includes your own personal webpage, with the opportunity to present yourself according to your own design, as well as your pages on websites like HELLO STAGE.

When tackling your online profiles, keep in mind the aspect of language. Classical music is a global market. While you will probably start your career in your home country, hopefully you will grow it quickly within your region and continent. If you aspire for an international career, you will need to have an English version of your digital presence. Making English your online presence's default language will make it easier and more compelling for people to reach out to you, and one in your native language will also retain your original audience. For the English speaking site, make sure that a professional editor and/or translator works on it, as your website also functions as a business card. Language mistakes look unprofessional, and with many freelancers providing these services at reasonable prices online, there is little reason not to invest in a well-written site.

Where to begin? The first thing you should do is reserve your URL - basically, your address on the internet. When somebody types in your URL (www.------.com) they will come to your website.

It is generally best to use your name as your URL. Take the violinist and conductor Julian Rachlin. His URL is www.julianrachlin.com. The ".com" is the so-called top level domain and the most well-known one. There are now endless top level domains of which ".com" was the first one. After ".com" country specific top level domains followed like ".uk" for the United Kingdom, ".de" for Germany and so on. Recently generic top level domains have followed including ".design", ".church" etc. The top level domain ".music" has been proposed while writing this book but is not available as of yet.

The easier your URL, the better, so your name followed by a relevant top level domain is usually a good bet. If the ".com" is still available, grab it! It is always the most common one.

Keep in mind that your URL should be easily memorable, so do not add your instrument or voice as it unnecessarily complicates things. If you have a double name, try to use a shorter form.

There are many places on the internet where you can register your URL. You can either purchase it at the same place where you will be hosting your website or separately from another site. We have found the following two domain registrants useful, easy to use, and with good services and pricing:

- www.joker.com

- www.networksolutions.com

However, there are thousands of others as well. You will find an updated list of domain name registrants on the website for this book: www.be-your-own-manager.com.

Once you've locked in your URL and registered it, you will have to decide where to host your website, meaning where the digital files which make up your website are actually placed. Yes, even in this digital age and the age of cloud computing, files need to be placed on a server somewhere in the world. For a website, this is called website hosting.

Several companies not only offer website hosting, but can also provide you with design templates to make website creation easier. They help you to get started on your own with easily assembled sites. A few of them include:

- Wordpress.com – www.wordpress.com – Originally developed as a hosting platform for blogs, it quickly has evolved into one of the most popular website hosting companies. It offers endless templates and plug-ins, but also requires some technical skills. If you choose to work with a web designer, they will probably use WordPress.

- Wix.com – www.wix.com – An easy to use website hosting and design platform. It is our recommendation for novice users. Pick a simple design and get started.

- Squarespace – www.squarespace.com – Another easy to use website hosting platform with many beautiful templates enabling you to create a website quickly.

There are many more webhosting providers out there with cool and beautiful templates, making it easy for you to create and maintain a website. Again, we keep a list of providers we like on the website of this book: www.be-your-own-manager.com.

HELLO STAGE – www.hellostage.com – The largest classical music community online where you can create your own standardized website with a personalized URL. The biggest benefit is that your website is not lost in the black hole of the internet, but rather is at a known place where the classical music community meets online. Furthermore, HELLO STAGE offers the unique benefit of being able to find musicians and singers based on the repertoire they play. It is the only place where one can look for a violinist playing the Ligeti violin concerto, and not only is one able to pull up all relevant violinists, but any other relevant information about these musicians can be found here too.

Though many of these platforms may offer free website hosting, it comes with the condition of heavy ad placement for their services on your page. Not only does this look unprofessional, speed and accessibility might be reduced as well. Therefore, we actually recommend paying between US$10 to US$25 per month for a subscription, rather than opting for the "free" package.

A few words of advice before you get started: rule #1 – keep it simple! Bettina and Bernhard have seen too many overly done webpages of classical musicians which are totally fancy, but basic information cannot easily be found. Having a straight-forward and simple design helps drastically. Make sure that your site can easily be navigated and that people can quickly find what they're looking for. Keep in mind that you lose a majority of your visitors with every click they need to make.

Another critical point in today's world is that your website needs to be mobile-enabled. The number of people surfing the web from their smartphone is increasing exponentially. You definitely lose a good part of your audience if your website does not work easily and nicely on a mobile device.

Lucky for us, most sites – especially most of the ones listed in the providers above – are already mobile ready and often done with responsive design. What does this mean? Responsive design is built into good websites, allowing the server where the website is hosted, to first assess what kind of device actually wants to view the content. Is it a laptop, a smart phone, a tablet, or another device? Depending on the viewing device, the server will then send the relevant data to the device so that it is beautifully displayed. That all works in the background of well-designed and programmed websites without the need for you to do anything.

The only question you might think of is to consider which content is relevant for being viewed on mobile devices. Many of the above website providers allow you to hide certain content on your website when viewed from a mobile device, as opposed to being able to see the entire website when checking from a desktop computer.

What content should you have on your website as a classical musician?

- Starting Page: With one quick glance, the starting page of your website should enable a visitor to grasp who you are and what you are about. A professional photo with your instrument should be the first image (see our Chapter PHOTOS AND VIDEOS). There should also be some short text of three to five clearly written sentences about you. Do not put your bio there! But write what makes you different in comparison to other musicians or use a quote that an esteemed colleague, teacher or mentor may have kindly provided you with. A great quote from an important paper also has a nice ring to it.

- If possible, displaying the next few events you are performing in, as well as the latest news are good visuals. But keep in mind that these should really be upcoming events and not ones from three years ago. Similarly, news really needs to be newsworthy.

- There are easy integration tools available for your social media channels if you use social media (which you should!). This can be a nice and easy option as opposed to a news section, but just keep in mind that your social media channels should only have professional content then. Having photos from your latest holiday, your cat, or your last meal turn up on your webpage looks unprofessional and takes away from your image.

- You might include a sign up form for your newsletter, as well as buttons to follow you on social media.

• Bio Section: Your bio should be long and detailed in this section. A long bio does not mean including your first concert when you were three years old (unless you performed at Carnegie Hall at that age!), but should certainly include the important steps of your career (see the Chapter BIOGRAPHY). Most importantly, make sure that your bio is up to date! You will need to update it every three to nine months. Also make sure that people can easily copy it for their program notes. Ideally, you should even provide them with a download of a shorter bio for program notes. One last note is that any bio should include the date it was last edited to ensure that out-of-date material is not being used.

• Repertoire Section: Having a repertoire section is important but tricky. First and foremost, your repertoire list really needs to be up to date. Be sure to only list pieces and roles you have performed recently and can perform with very short notice.

- For instrumentalists and conductors, promoters will want to know what you have actually performed in concert where, when and with whom. Just having prepared a concerto but never having played it is not enough. So make sure to link repertoire with actual performances, as it is done on HELLO STAGE. Instrumentalists might add introductory text to their repertoire section about their favorite repertoire without listing all detailed works, but perhaps including their favorite composers.

- For singers, the repertoire list should include all full roles which you have sung, with the information of when, where and with whom you have performed, or which you have studied and are ready to perform.

• Events Section: The events section should be broken into previous and upcoming events.

- For previous events, only include the ones of importance. Important events include the stepping stones of your career, when you played with a major orchestra (the biggest one for the time being), a well-known or upcoming conductor, or at a highly reputable venue or festival. As you go along, you might want to revisit this list and erase the ones you have outgrown.

- For upcoming events you can include any. This helps people attending or wanting to attend your next concert or opera performance. However, you might decide not to list a place you might be trying out new repertoire. Often it can make sense to choose an out of the way place for your first time with a new big concerto or a major role you are actually preparing for a major venue.

- Reviews: Obviously if you have reviews, it's great to put them on your webpage. However, be aware of different copyright laws. Unfortunately, there is not one uniform worldwide rule on this matter. Many legislations prohibit you from copying whole articles onto your website, but it is often ok to quote two or three sentences from a review. In any case, always provide the correct source and a link to the full article. You might also ask the publication if you can use the review. Some papers in the US will comply for a modest fee. If in doubt, do check with a copyright lawyer or a musicians' association in your country.

- Media Section: The media section should contain photos as well as videos.

  - Photos should be formatted such that they can be easily looked at without taking too long to load. It is normally best for photos not to have more than 500 kb in terms of file size. Choose a variety of photos ranging from professional shots to some showing you on stage. But don't overdo it! Five to twelve photos are fine. You might provide a link to download high-resolution photos for print. Do not forget to add copyright information and credits for the photographer. It also might be advisable to have both a color and a black and white headshot that is downloadable so that promoters do not have to get in touch if they need your photo for the program book or other marketing material.

  - Videos are really important today. Promoters want to see you "in action" and get a feeling for how you are on stage.

Keep in mind that people's attention spans have shrunk to one minute, even though it was three minutes just a few years ago. Having a variety of performance videos, best shot live, is helpful. You might also add a feature about you. (See the Chapter PHOTOS AND VIDEOS) Videos can be hosted on YouTube or another video platform such as Vimeo and can be linked to your webpage. Many website hosting services offer plugins which make it easy to add videos to your website.

- Contact: It goes without saying to make sure that people can actually contact you. The contact page should be easily found and very, very clearly structured. It should start with your main contact – this can be you or your manager. If you do not have a manager yet, put down your work email address.

  - When putting an email address on a webpage, we recommend writing it in a bit of a different form such as "office(at)hellostage.com" as opposed to using the actual "@." This makes it harder for spammers to pick off your email address. It is advisable to use separate email addresses for your website than your main email in order to manage spam. Nevertheless, be sure to check both regularly.

  - An alternative is to program a little contact form. If someone fills it out, it will still feed directly into your email box, but again, it makes it more difficult for spammers to find your email address. However, visitors are not always comfortable with this option and may be discouraged from contacting you.

  - The question of whether or not to advertise your telephone number is a difficult one. If you have a phone answering service or can use the office number of your manager, that is most likely a fine option. However, advertising your mobile number may lead to a lot of unwanted calls and you may not want the loss of privacy. On the other hand, it does make it easier for promoters to contact you if they need a quick replacement. A good compromise is to set up an exclusive work phone number through a free option like Google Voice and have it routed to your cell phone.

- News Section: If you have regular news, at least monthly, having a news section might add to the attractiveness of your site, but is not absolutely necessary. If you do not want to write news regularly, skip this section.

If you do not want to develop your website on your own, there are many good website designers and developers out there who can do it for you. Go with someone who has worked with classical musicians before, as they will know best what is relevant and will understand the world of classical music.

If you do commission someone else to do your website, make sure that they use an easy-to-use content management system and that you will be able to understand how to use it yourself. Otherwise you will have to go back for every update and small change you want to make. An easily accessible and understandable content management system should let you change photos, text, add concerts, news, etc. For example, on HELLO STAGE, we allow you to update events on your HELLO STAGE page directly, which are then automatically updated on your website, making website upkeep much easier.

The differences in cost when commissioning a website can be huge. Be sure that you understand exactly what you are commissioning and what is or is not included. The elements you need to consider are:

- The design itself

- Photo and graphical material

- Fonts

- Hosting

- Content management

A typical webpage for a classical musician or ensemble can cost anywhere between US$1,000 and US$10,000.

We feel we should mention one important red flag in this whole process. You would be surprised by how many webpages of some very well-known artists have been hacked in the last few years. Sometimes it ended up being the HELLO STAGE team making its members aware that their personal website was hacked. Creating and maintaining a website in today's world is significantly more complex than just having a nice design, so you should maintain awareness regarding security and protecting your privacy and materials.

A good alternative or useful addition to creating your own website is to seek out a platform similar to HELLO STAGE. There are a growing number of such platforms which allow you to create your own page. Many of them provide you with better security at a much lower cost than having your own webpage. One of the major benefits of HELLO STAGE, besides the size of its community, is that promoters and orchestras can find you based on your repertoire. They can, for example, look up who played Rodion Shchedrin's Concerto for Piano and Orchestra No. 4 and will find that pianist Anika Vavic has performed it several times, among others with Maestro Valery Gergiev.

One last bit of advice - some people think that having a lot of hits on your website will make a huge difference in your career. This assumption would be correct for a consumer product, but is not necessarily so for a classical musician. The only thing that counts for you as a classical musician is having the relevant people find you and your website. The number of hits is irrelevant, so don't bother buying hits for your site. Yes, that is something you can do, but definitely not something to worry about!

[7]

SOCIAL MEDIA STRATEGY

SOME MIGHT SAY THAT social media has become the new-found obsession of the 21st century, with people posting every detail of their lives publicly, spending more time with virtual friends than real ones, and wasting inordinate amounts of time online. While aspects of these statements may certainly hold true, social media also has many benefits. Utilized positively, social media can provide tangible pathways to connect with your audience, and to enter into a conversation with people interested in your career. We will discuss both: an overview of social media, as well as recommended and proven strategies for classical musicians when it comes to this new market disruptor.

What is social media? Simply put, it encompasses various platforms that allow you to broadcast personal and business content to either a more general public or just to selected people. More importantly, it enables you to engage with people who have interests closely aligned with what you are doing. Your social media audience can be public, self-selected, or more narrowly limited, depending on the platform. The biggest platform by far is Facebook, initially founded in 2004 as a way for college students to communicate with each other. Other platforms then followed, which we will discuss in more detail later in this chapter. The most important factor to keep in mind for all of this is that you will want to create relevant content so that you can grow an audience interested in this content and thereby you.

Social media has grown so quickly and so powerfully that you should not make the mistake of thinking that posting on social media is the same as disseminating a newsletter in terms of reach. It will depend on the size of your audience, but it will also depend on the way it is tagged, archived and accessed within the greater system. Sometimes your reach may be much greater than you might have expected, especially if your content goes viral, such as it did when the Al Bustan Festival Orchestra played a variation on the Darth Vader Star Wars theme during rehearsal as a practical joke (Enjoy: www.facebook.com/hellostage/videos/779491408854744/). Other times, because of the exponential nature of daily growth in content, your posts can just get lost in the jungle. Platforms have had to develop ways to make all the content manageable for its readers, leading most to use some kind of filter algorithms. Twitter tried, unsuccessfully, to introduce filtering in 2015, but they were quickly booed down by their users so they have stopped for now. What this means is that timelines on Twitter are so full now that readers easily miss Tweets if posts are not published around the time users happen to look on their Twitter feed. So essentially your content will only be visible to a fraction of your followers on any social media platform due to algorithms and the amount of content posted every day.

When dealing with social media, first it is important to consider which platforms suit you best. There is no need to be present across every single platform unless you want to become a professional social media manager. Pick one to three platforms you like best and use them frequently. Posting regularly is more critical than being present on multiple platforms. Of course, "regular" means different things for each platform, but we will go into further detail on this later. Regardless, you should be aware that you should post several times a week, and often up to once a day in order for you to build a relevant social media presence.

Keep in mind that one of the biggest brands in the world, Apple, does not use social media at all. So while using social media is not necessarily required if you are a really huge brand, it's worth checking out for the rest of us who want to develop name recognition like Apple.

When posting, try to be aware of influential factors such as time. Obviously, it does not make sense to post anything if most of your audience is asleep. Pick times where the majority of your followers are online. Good times are around 10am when people start their days and quickly log into social media for a spot check; around lunch time; and around 5pm as people launch into their evenings.

SOCIAL MEDIA CONTENT

Above all, your actual content is the most crucial part of the equation. Think about what kind of content is relevant for your audience; in fact, formulate five key themes that characterize you that you want to get across to your audience. Pack them into stories, and do not just repeat similar posts. Avoid the braggadocios posts, since no one wants to read about how great you are. You want your audience to understand you and see things from your point of view, and if you can do this successfully, they will think you're great anyway without the need for a humblebrag post. Genuine excitement and authenticity will help you establish this more than anything.

When developing a content strategy, start with yourself. Early in this book we (See PERSONAL BRAND) wrote about the characteristics which make you unique. This can be the repertoire you are playing, the partners you like to play with, your preferred genre, a certain kind of tone or interpretation. Define this for your content strategy as well, and consider what content fits. Content will include you performing, your thoughts on composers and pieces in that area, etc. but can also include people or places that inspire you in those areas. You can post about your teacher, about artists who have inspired you, about relevant places and discoveries.

For example, let's say that you are a pianist currently focusing on Johann Sebastian Bach. Your content should not only include yourself playing Bach, but also some of your greatest inspirations. This could be videos from other pianists such as Glenn Gould, or if you prefer not to be compared with other pianists, you could link to the Bach Cello Solo Suites with Pablo Casals. You could also post what Nikolaus Harnoncourt and others have said about Bach's music, upload pictures from the places Bach lived (hopefully with you in them!), and work related to his manuscripts and more.

Another theme could be focused around your instrument. Stories of instruments are much more fascinating for outsiders than you might think. Harpsichordist Medea Bindewald (www.hellostage.com/Medea-Bindewald) regularly posts about old keyboard instruments she has discovered. The back history of your violin might be fascinating. Who played it before? Where and how did you find it?

You will also want to keep things personal. This does not mean you have to give up your privacy, nor do we recommend that you freely share your private life with the world. But there are probably aspects of yourself that are fun which you feel comfortable sharing. This might be something like your love of good food or humorous jokes, like the ones conductor Paavo Järvi (www.instagram.com/pjarvi/) shares. An especially nice way of letting people peek a bit into your personal life is done well by pianist Simone Dinnerstein who regularly posts videos of her dog Daisy listening – or not listening! – to her practice... (www.facebook.com/simonedinnerstein).

The Arcis Saxophon Quartett has made it a habit to take a photo from the stage out into the audience and posting this every time they have a concert (www.hellostage.com/Arcis-Saxophon-Quartett). Hillary Hahn speaks from the viewpoint of her violin case, who posts about the trips with its owner (www.twitter.com/violincase).

Classical music aficionados love to peek behind the curtains. There is a reason why you can buy backstage passes for pop concerts, so why not use this same mindset and apply it to your social media? Post a photo showing the stage doors you walked through, the view from the green rooms, or what the view of the stage looks like from behind the stage. A fun example is entrepreneur and activist Ali Mahlodji, who always posts selfies from his speaking engagements with his audience (www.facebook.com/alimahlodji). Another example of a smart social media user is a young and passionate tennis player, Maggie, who utilizes her Instagram account as a journal (www.instagram.com/maggie.tennis).

Speaking about your upcoming concerts, next album, workshops, masterclasses, crowdfunding, and so on is important, but you will only reach followers with these kinds of news if the rest of your social media content is relevant and enjoyable for your audience, so that it is not seen as pure self-promotion.

Violin grandmaster Itzhak Perlman (www.hellostage.com/itzhakperlman) centers his social media around:

- Being a fan of the New York Mets

- Humor, including never being afraid to make jokes about himself

- Caring for people, be it his support to the End Polio Campaign or people being hit by natural disasters

- Earlier recordings and upcoming concerts

Similarly choose three to five themes besides announcing your concerts and such. Describe them in a note to yourself so that you can be clear for yourself, then work on collecting examples of your themes. These will form the base of a content plan and make your social media activities significantly more interesting. Revisit your themes regularly every three to six months and update them if necessary.

Social Media Channels

While brainstorming on themes to use in a content plan, you will need to decide which social media platforms you really want to use. Keep in mind that simple content duplication is not a good strategy since each social media channel has its own characteristics. Understanding each and developing content accordingly is crucial for your social media success.

Facebook

Facebook (www.facebook.com) is by far the biggest social media channel, with 1.7 billion users worldwide. It is the one platform you probably should be on, although there are artists who decide against it. On Facebook, it is easy enough to start with a personal page. With a personal profile, you are allowed up to 5,000 so-called friends. People can also follow you without being a friend, if you allow this option on your page. Additionally, you can create a "Page". This is like a microsite that anyone can see and which is often used by artists, orchestras, ensembles and organizations. There are no limits on how many "likes" you can have on your Page.

When you log on to Facebook as a user, you will see your News-feed, which will contain the posts of your friends as well as of Pages you have liked. However, you will quickly learn that your feed will not contain all the posts from your friends and the Pages you have liked because Facebook filters your Newsfeed heavily. If you go to your list of your friends and click on one you haven't heard from in awhile, you will see that they did put up posts, but that it was not displayed on your Newsfeed. Facebook argues that they want to make your Newsfeed relevant, so they therefore continuously work on their algorithms to decide what to show you and what not to. Facebook uses your behavior on their platform to determine what they think is relevant for you or not. You will see more posts from people you have exchanged messages with than from others, and you will also see posts from people who have looked at your profile recently, etc.

If you are posting from your Page, you cannot expect that a standard post is seen by more than 10% of the people who have liked your Page, on average. Actually Facebook will show you on your Page, though not on your personal Profile, how many people you reached with your post. This can sometimes be a bit shocking.

The reason for the throttling is because you can pay Facebook to boost your post so that more people see it. This a decision you should consider very carefully. On the one hand, Facebook offers you amazing targeting options to send your posts to people who really should see it. For example, if you are playing a concert in Boston, you can boost a post so that only people interested in piano in Boston can see it. Spending US$1-10 on a post can make a huge difference. But you also need to be aware that once you start paying for posts, Facebook will want you to continue doing so. This means that if you discontinue spending money, you will often see the reach of your posts fall dramatically.

Facebook offers the widest variety of content that can be posted, from a short text, to longer notes, photos, albums, videos, etc. From time to time, Facebook introduces new features. For example, in 2016 they introduced Facebook Live, allowing people to video stream live from anywhere using their smartphones. Whenever Facebook launches such a new feature, they will push the content created with this new feature stronger than other content, so it is a good idea to keep an eye out for new features and try them out when they are launched.

With Facebook, you should post almost daily. Having a Page, as opposed to a personal profile, has several benefits beyond detailed statistics about people who liked your page and read your posts. One of them is that you can actually schedule posts. This allows you to create your posts ahead of time and then schedule them to be posted on various days during the coming week, ensuring that you post at optimal times when the most people are likely to read your posts.

TWITTER

Twitter (www.twitter.com) is probably the second widest social media channel used with over 300 million users worldwide. However, the use of Twitter is very geographically specific, being mainly used in North America and much less in other parts of the world. For example, Twitter is only used by 7% of social media users in Germany versus 17% in the USA, according to the Global Web Index from Q4 2015. In Europe, the UK is more into Twitter than into Facebook. The growth of Twitter has also slowed down.

Twitter started as a short text blogging platform. You have up to 140 characters to write a short note, called Tweets, and share it with the world. Lately you can add photos and videos to it. Because of this heavy reliance on text, Twitter worked really well before having broadband access on your smartphone became common.

An important element of Twitter, similar to Instagram, is the concept of hashtags. Hashtags "#" allow users to find content based on these subject-based markings. If someone is interested in classical music, he might look for #classicalmusic. By clicking on that hashtag, he can then access all Tweets marked with that hashtag. Hashtagging is a great way to cross-reference your posts and to win a greater following on Twitter.

We at HELLO STAGE introduced the hashtag #classicalbuzz on Twitter and Instagram to strengthen the classical music community. Using such a hashtag allows you to reach people who are interested in your subject matter. You can also search for hashtags and like and comment on what other people are posting. Remember, social media is about conversations, and not just about pushing your own content.

Twitter is great if you are a witty writer and can put your thoughts down in only a few words. It is also good to get across basic information, e.g. an upcoming concert. Some companies use Twitter purely as an information channel for support and technical issues.

But Twitter is also work-intensive. Because of the thousands of Tweets every day – or better, every minute – you need to post several times a day to cut above the fray. Our recommendation is to Tweet at least three to four times. The Twitter algorithm will punish you if you post the same content, but slightly varied content is always possible.

Tweetdeck (tweetdeck.twitter.com), a software now owned by Twitter, helps you to schedule your Tweets. Tweetdeck allows you to plan all your tweeting in one day for a whole week or even longer. This makes the implementation of your social media plan much easier.

INSTAGRAM

Instagram (www.instagram.com) has now become one of the fastest growing social media channels with more than 400 million users. Instagram was originally designed to share photos, but you can now share video clips, as well as post Instagram Stories, which are 24 hour only, disappearing posts, like Snapchat. All posts allow space for captions as well, which many users load up with hashtags so that their posts can be found. Instagram is primarily a smartphone-based app. Until recently, you could not even use it on a web browser on a computer. Instagram is really optimized to take a photo quickly with your smartphone, edit it with great editing tools, and share it.

Many artists find Instagram to be their preferred social media platform, as it is easy to use and very spontaneous. Shooting photos from the hall you are performing in, your dinner after the concert, or before going on stage to take your bow are fun snapshots. Venues, Orchestras and opera houses have started to use Instagram as well, and will often hand over their account to the artist of the week, a singer or an orchestra member, to guest post, which is not only great fun, but also a very good way to engage the artist's fans with their own account.

Similar to Twitter, hashtags help build a followership beyond your immediate fans, and are probably used even more strongly on Instagram than on Twitter. You can use up to 20 different hashtags per post. Be creative! Whenever you are typing a hashtag, Instagram shows you the number of posts that have already used the same hashtag. Aim for popular ones! And use #classicalbuzz!

GOOGLE

Google (plus.google.com) tried to get into the social media space strongly with Google+. Although, as you would expect from Google, it has some awesome features, we have not really seen Google+ taking off. It is probably best leave it out of your considerations for the time being, as it has not really taken off.

LinkedIn

LinkedIn (www.linkedin.com) is more of a professional community than a social media channel. Founded as a network for professionals, especially engineers, managers, accountants, etc., it provides a space to create your own microsite, very close to an online curriculum vitae. Recruiters were the first to start using LinkedIn strongly to find talent. People looking for jobs ensured that they were on it and grew their network. Users can now post news and updates, participate in group discussions, and even chat. LinkedIn has around 100 million users.

There are several groups related to classical music on LinkedIn. You might want to check them out, but we do not see it as a major social media channel for classical musicians specifically. The purpose of LinkedIn was to create a network for business professionals, not classical musicians. Non-members can hardly follow you there.

Other Channels

Lately there is a whole group of new channels which mostly come from the private messaging arena, and they are growing fast.

In China, you cannot avoid WeChat. With more than 700 million users, almost all of China is on it. Initially started as a communication platform, it is now a hybrid messaging and social media platform. You can only use it on smartphones. You can have your own page with public updates or message just your friends.

One of the fastest growing hybrid platforms is Snapchat. According to Forbes (www.bloomberg.com/news/articles/2016-06-02/snapchat-passes-twitter-in-daily-usage) it had 150 million daily users in

June 2016, more than Twitter. The demographics for Snapchat are quite interesting, as it is mostly used by teenagers and early tweens. They were attracted to Snapchat because photos could only be seen for up to 10 seconds by their friends and could not be downloaded. After many stories of younger generations having trouble finding jobs because of their party photos on Facebook, this became an attractive alternative medium. Photos could be easily edited with several fun elements from text to animal face filters, etc.

Snapchat went on to introduce stories, which are only visible for 24 hours. They allowed brands and celebrities to share photos with their followers, which gave a fleeting glimpse into someone's day, but felt intimate for that exact same reason. Because of the demographics, many jumped on the opportunity, and some users have millions of followers. Geofiltering makes Snapchat even more interesting. These reasons have prompted some organizations in classical music to experiment with Snapchat.

Though there are many more social media channels and hybrid platforms, our advice is to only use the ones you are familiar with, which are easy for you to use, and which have a relevant reach among the people you want to target.

SOCIAL MEDIA PLAN

If you want to use social media to advance your career, invest time into developing a social media plan. You might even pay for advice from specialists who can help you operationalize it.

We recommend a weekly plan. The plan is a simple table with the days of the week on top and the times of the day to the left. Add a column each day for the two to three social media channels you want to actively use. Then assign each of your up-to-five content subjects, one color. This will give you a colorful table.

Before you get started, do consider where most of your fans are located. In North America? In Europe? In Asia? Or in more than one of these regions? This is important to understand for the timing of your posts. In the example above, you can see the grey areas for which part of the day it is in each region. So, if you are based in North America, post only during those times when North America is awake. Good times are mornings before people go to work, during lunch time, and early evenings after work.

Pick one day every week to sit down and do your social media scheduling for the seven days following. Start by jotting down an idea per content subject, then link a delivery mode to each content idea, which can be a text, a photo, a video, etc. Some content ideas will have multiple delivery modes. Begin to then distribute these ideas with the relevant delivery mode into your social media plan, choosing which channels/platforms to use when and for what. Remember that you can actually repeat the same story, perhaps with a different twist, throughout the week. This can actually take up to four hours to fully plan out a week and all its subsequent content.

After all that theory, let us share an example with you. We will present an exemplary social media plan for the Korean flutist Jasmine Choi (www.hellostage.com/jasmine-choi). Jasmine is an outstanding virtuoso on the flute. She lives in Austria at Lake Constance and regularly plays in Europe, the US and Korea. She has recorded several albums, most of them for Sony. Sometimes she joins orchestras, such as the Estonian Festival Orchestra.

Her content subjects are clearly defined:

- Her upcoming "Love in Paris" tour in Korea

- Her musical friend guitarist Ben Beirs, whom she has just performed with in Paris

- Her recent CD of the Telemann Files

- Her love for wine

So the stories for a typical week could look as follows:

- Love in Paris: Promote upcoming concerts

    - Photo of brochures in concert halls

    - Photo of reception after one of her earlier concerts

    - Short video of her introducing the program

    - Dates of the tour

- Guitarist Ben Beirs: Review of recent concerts

    - Video from a recent concert

    - Video of Ben teaching yoga, which has become very important to him

- Album Telemann Files: Background story to the CD

    - A short story of who she was thinking about for the B minor fantasy

- Love for Wine: Her recent discovery of the Valdonica wines from Tuscany

    - Photo of a wine bottle

    - Text about what she likes about the wine and some background to the winery

Suddenly she has content that can easily fill her weekly plan, has diversity, and shows different aspects of her persona.

In addition to the weekly content planning and scheduling session, you should still be spending roughly 30 minutes a day on social media. During that time, share the content of your friends, of the places you have performed or will perform at, or of areas relevant to your content subjects. Like what other people are posting and leave comments as well. You might even do some spontaneous Tweets or Instagram posts, but focus on sharing, liking and commenting.

BUILDING YOUR SOCIAL MEDIA FOLLOWING

So how exactly do you build your social media following? This doesn't happen on its own, not even for the biggest names. It requires work. When you are new to social media, start with one or two channels only.

First of all, put your new social media channels on your website and on your newsletters. Wherever you already have a digital presence, add the symbols for the social media channels and link them to your accounts.

Then start finding and following your friends and colleagues on their respective channels. Start liking and sharing their content. Also, find concert halls, orchestras, music schools, etc. which all use social media and follow them. You will see that you can quickly build your following.

There exists an unspoken rule in social media, which is that if someone follows you, you normally follow back.

On Instagram and Twitter, anyone can follow you if you have a public account. Also on your Facebook Page, everyone can follow you. To become friends on your personal Facebook account with others, there is a request and approval process, as is similarly done with private accounts on Instagram.

Wherever there is a request and accept process in place, we highly recommend not accepting just anyone. If you know the person, sure, that is easy. However, if you don't know them, look at their profiles, see if you share mutual friends, look at what their interests are, and also check that the accounts look legitimate. Only then should you approve a friend or contact request, if you feel comfortable with what you see. Because there are many fake accounts out there, and a few with even criminal intent, it is smart to be careful.

Although the practice of buying followers does exist, we obviously do not recommend doing so as it undermines your credibility. Today it is actually very easy to analyze where your followers come from, and it looks dubious if most of your followers come from a country you have never even set foot in.

Sharing content and using hashtags such as #classicalbuzz for example, is a most powerful way to gain followers. These acts help the whole community, and therefore you as well. It builds up your social media credibility and supports you in growing your audience.

Keep in mind that you will want to keep your social media activities manageable. When setting up your social media presence, you might initially have time to do it and enjoy the process. But keep in mind that more stressful periods filled with lots of other work will be coming, where you may not have time to feed five hungry social media channels. Set yourself modest targets in the beginning, as you can always grow your presence later if you wish to do so.

Last but not least, besides all the serious advice in this chapter, keep it light and fun! Doing social media should not be another chore you add to your daily schedule, but a joy – the joy of sharing your passion for classical music. Being active on social media is not just advertising. It is entering into a conversation with a huge community, and listening is just as important as speaking, where you are also apt to learn many intriguing things about the world around you.

[8]

SELLING YOURSELF

YOU'VE GOTTEN YOUR NAME out there. Promoters, presenters, orchestras have started noticing you. In order to land engagements and not just picking them up as they come your way by chance, you need to start selling. Selling means going after real deals, i.e. offering yourself up and closing the ones that seem right. This is not done quickly and may happen less often than you like, but regardless, selling requires time, effort, and a thoughtful process. In this chapter we would like to suggest a proven sales process based on what you have already learned thus far in this book, and give you a structured way to go about it. The idea of selling is probably uncomfortable to you, as it is for many people, but it is a necessary part of the game. Hopefully the following pointers will help you to feel more at ease concerning the process.

Why is it even necessary to sell yourself as an artist? Isn't it enough to just be a really good musician? Unfortunately, this is not the case. Being an outstanding musician only qualifies you to participate in the Olympics. It does not get you on a team or win you a medal. For that, you need to be successful salesperson as well. Even if you have good management they only can support you and you actually have to do a lot of selling yourself. Your management will handle more of the organizational elements, do follow-ups, etc., but you will always be your own strongest salesperson.

This mind shift when thinking about selling yourself is important. You are not begging for engagements, even if some promoters may try to put you in that position. You are a great musician and have something unique to offer. You give the promoter and their audiences the chance to experience this for themselves. This is not to make you arrogant, but to provide you with self-esteem and a bit of self-confidence.

Before we address what you should be sending to promoters and orchestras, let's look at the theory of selling:

THE SALES FUNNEL – A PRACTICAL WAY OF ORGANIZING YOUR SALES EFFORTS

Selling is actually, more than anything else, a well-designed process. You might have the best product, but if you do not have a sales process, nobody will buy it. You would be surprised to learn that even big brands like Coca Cola, with a seemingly ubiquitous product, utilize very specific sales tools and processes. A 2015 Harvard Study found that companies with an effective sales process had a 15% increase in sales (www.hbr.org/2015/01/companies-with-a-formal-sales-process-generate-more-revenue). This even hit 28% if they followed certain principles. Why not apply these findings to your career?

We all know how a funnel works. You pour lots of liquid into it and get one focused continuous stream out. This is also the basic principle of a sales funnel: you pour lots of real sales leads into it to achieve a constant stream of engagements. The trick is to manage that funnel correctly at each step along the way, in order to achieve the best and most efficient results for everyone involved.

The first step in creating a sales funnel is to categorize the different layers of the funnel. You place your contacts and relevant organizations in these layers, and by working on them over time, move them slowly down the funnel until you are booked by them.

The process starts with leads and ends with engagements. In between, the layers comprise the process in which you effectively manage your contacts. We suggest the following layers:

- **Leads:** This layer includes all the organizations that could possibly engage you for a concert or a recital. If you are just starting out, these will include the (smaller) promoters in your area, and not necessarily Carnegie Hall. Make sure that your leads list is relevant to the stage at where you are at in your career.

- **General Interest:** Here you should include all contacts who have expressed a general interest in you. Make notes and detail as much as possible with regard to their interest. Did it have to do with a specific repertoire, a festival they were thinking of, or a specific event? A good idea is to make notes of each conversation you have with a new general interest, so that you don't forget what may have sparked an interest, rather than just remembering that you had a nice encounter after somebody else's concert or where you happened to meet.

- **Concrete Interest:** Once contacts from the general interest list have expressed a concrete interest in engaging you, they move into this layer. At this point you should already have an idea about the season they are looking at and/or a program they might be looking for, but likely without many more details than that.

- **Penciled:** Once the interests of the above layer has become so concrete that you are asked to hold dates, i.e. to pencil them in, then you can move the contact to this layer.

- **Engagements:** Finally, hopefully, many of the contacts from the above funnel through to concrete engagements with signed contracts.

To successfully manage a funnel, you need to be able to progressively move contacts from one layer to the next, but this needs more than a simple address book. It will make you more effective if you are able to connect contacts and emails sent and received, to opportunities in your sales funnel. We recommend using available software solutions, as your sales process will become much more efficient and professional once you learn how to use them.

We introduce a few platforms here. Find the one that is commonly available, easy to use on your smartphone, and most intuitive for you. Ask around what others may use, try things out, and find what suits your needs best.

- Daylite by Marketcircle (www.marketcircle.com/daylite): We at HELLO STAGE have been using Daylite from day one. It was the perfect tool for us, and has gotten even better, as it now provides a good cloud solution. Daylite connects contacts to opportunities, projects, etc., and has a good email plug-in. You can use it easily on your smartphone, as well as on your computer. Not only are all emails accessible by contact, but you can also categorize each contact, link it to opportunities, create a sales funnel, etc.

- Insightly (www.insightly.com): Insightly is another sales and project management tool that comes, in its simple form, for free. It allows you to schedule emails automatically and send mass emails.

- Zoho CRM (www.zoho.com): Another very popular tool is Zoho CRM, although this platform might already offer too many options for classical musicians. It has basically the same features as the solutions mentioned above, and starts at US$15 per month per user.

So what's the best way to get started? First, set aside a few days to sort out your contacts and start setting up your sales funnel. Collect all professional contacts you've met along the way and gather whatever you can find anywhere – promoters who engaged you, conductors and orchestra managers you auditioned for, presenters you met, orchestras you were in contact with or met while taking part in a competition, etc. Go through your emails to see which contacts were important for you (sort by sender instead of by date, and you can get this done faster).

Then start categorizing each contact according to the sales funnel and the database segments explained in the Chapter MARKETING. A promoter who invited you three years ago but not since would end up in the Leads layer, despite you having performed there. But you could categorize him as an Acquaintance, probably at the decision maker level, and also mark him as a promoter. You should also add an extra category to make note of the fact that you have already performed there.

If you are currently discussing a concert with an orchestra (or a recital with a promoter) for one of their future seasons, this should end up in the Concrete Interest Layer. And so on.

Although this can be quite tedious work if you have to work through all your contacts, it will help you so much so it is well worth it.

Once you are set up, you can start working with the funnel regularly. We suggest spending a few hours on it every week so that it then becomes a productive routine. In these hours, as you go through all the contacts in your funnel and see what the last action was, it helps to determine what the next task should be. Connecting a task list to your funnel makes it even stronger.

To continue with the above example, let's consider this promoter you played for three years ago. He is currently in the Lead Layer, but the question is, how can you move him to the General Interest Layer?

We first suggest researching or asking for their planning priorities over the next coming seasons. See what you can offer that fits their priorities, then drop them an email with a concrete suggestion that aligns with those said priorities. In this email, you can also briefly mention your latest CD, a big concert you've just played, send the latest review, or other news which may be relevant to the promoter. You can link a task to the email to follow up in two weeks.

You can work this same approach for the orchestra you currently have been holding discussions with about doing something together in the next coming seasons. What does it take to move them from the Concrete Interest Layer to the Penciled one? Perhaps they already have a conductor in mind whom they would like you to work with and you might happen to know him or her. Then you could reach out to the conductor informally. They might have even penciled in a period with the conductor. Discuss with them and try to get their agreement to pencil you in for this period as well. Again, link it with relevant tasks on your task list. A key tactic at this stage is to find out what the other side is thinking, rather than you telling them what you have in mind for your upcoming projects. However, if they happen to lack inspiration, it is of course a good idea to make suggestions yourself.

One piece of advice: in case their repertoire ideas do not meet your preferences at all, it is worth bringing this matter up. If they are interested in you as an artist, they will find it worthwhile to wait to find the right circumstances for you, rather than forcing you into a piece that does not suit you. The result could be that you would be unhappy with the "wrong" concerto and not deliver a performance you are capable of. This could then domino into an unhappy presenter who could likely put you on the backburner for a re-engagement. Sometimes it's just better to wait, despite the temptation to jump at the opportunity. You have already moved them to the edge of the Concrete Interest Layer, so they will eventually fall into the Penciled one!

This is how you should proceed through every contact with a general or more concrete opportunity to perform. Do it every week to see where you are on each opportunity. This certainly does not mean that you contact everyone in the funnel every single week, but it gives you a feeling as to what you should follow up on when. Generally speaking, you should contact people in the Leads Layer only two to four times a year to keep them up-to-date with your activities, which should trigger their imagination, while you might be in much more frequent contact with a promoter with whom you have already penciled in a date, to flesh out all the details.

This orderly process allows you to create a coordinated and professional follow up on each and every opportunity. It will often happen that you might move a contact or opportunity back up the funnel instead of down for various reasons. Being able to access the history of what you did when, and what was discussed, is one of the secrets of selling successfully.

The benefit of adopting this process is not only that it will help enable you to get more engagements, but the industry will also regard you as a professional on the business side, and this will make your collaboration with a manager easier in the future and more efficient for everyone involved.

In classical music just as in any other industry, repeat sales are a major driver of financial success. When people like your performance, they are inclined to re-invite you. In Europe, promoters have a tendency to pass one or two seasons in between your return. However, in other places promoters might want to build upon your success by bringing you back quicker so that you can build up your own following in that area. Find out about these general policies of the promoters and structure your selling activities accordingly. In any case, efficiently managing your sales process will help create and manage these repeat sales – or re-invitations – and make your life a lot easier.

The repeat sales opportunity actually starts when you arrive at a new venue, even before having performed. Building up a personal relationship with the artistic planning staff and potentially the artistic director is important, as is having a good reputation with all the people working at the venue. This critical part is the bit of sales you will never get rid of, even despite having a wonderful manager who may take care of making sure that your calendar is full.

Remember that word travels fast within an organization regarding artists who are a pleasure to work with backstage versus the ones who are much more difficult to handle. Our recommendation would be not only to aim at the Intendant of the venue (a mistake that a lot of younger artists make), but to get to know the rest of the team - they are talented people as well who will soon climb the ladder and be in a position to invite artists, or move to another venue or orchestra.

Your time at a venue allows you to learn more about it, about their planning cycle, their planning focus, and decision-making. Use that opportunity and take your detailed notes so that you will remember a year later.

If a concert went well, there is no harm in asking the artistic planning team about their ideas and plans for the future in general. You should be able to propose projects based on their programming focus if you've done your homework here.

You would be surprised to hear how often an artist who has just played a fantastic classical concert with a great chamber orchestra might suggest doing a big romantic piece next – which calls for a full-blown symphony orchestra and not a chamber orchestra. Or how often a musician might propose to play Johann Sebastian Bach the next time, after just having performed at a contemporary music festival. You always want to keep in mind the decision maker's needs, wants and focuses first.

Last but not least, carefully select the communications channels with all your leads. We know of promoters who still work with fax machines – yes, those antique machines where you first type up a letter, print it out, then put it in the machine and it comes out somewhere else around the world. While email is the most used tool, calling people to follow up sometimes works well too. If you are in town and you have already some contact established with leads in your sales funnel, you can always ask for a meeting. If people are far up in the funnel, asking them for a meeting - not to sell a project - but to seek their advice is a little trick, which often opens many doors, leading to more introductions and perhaps even invitations. Be very, very careful with texting people or using their mobile numbers even if you have them. This is often seen as very personal, and people might be annoyed if artists invade what is considered private space.

Effective selling is a process that requires consistency and regularity. If you do it right, it will boost your career, therefore it is a weekly time investment well worth it.

[9]

PROGRAMMING

YOU MIGHT WONDER WHY we ask that you take a closer look at programming, as it feels truly like an artistic issue and much less one of management. However, there is a certain management aspect that creeps in because you have to ask yourself: how sellable is this program that you have in mind? Or if you would like to be more challenging, what else might you need to provide with the program in order to get attention? Your programs will always need to grab the attention of promoters and be sellable to them. But then, and this does not make it easier, the promoters need to believe that they, too, can sell your program ideas to their audiences.

We don't consider a sellable program to be something lighthearted or one only consisting of Mozart, Beethoven and Haydn to make it "easier" for the consumer. Neither do we believe that putting together all the "highlights" of popular classical music will get the attention of promoters. Just like you, we squirm a little at these ideas. Nevertheless, the idea of being sellable is still one to contend with, if you want promoters to work with you.

When sending in proposals, be aware that there always exists a carefully considered planning process on part of the many promoters and orchestras. They have regular artistic planning meetings where worthwhile ideas are put forth and discussed by all the team members. At the Wiener Konzerthaus, we had these meetings at least every other week.

When Bettina was working at The Deutsche Kammerphilharmonie Bremen, they got together every second month with a planning committee, consisting of two players, a musicologist, the managing director, and Bettina herself as artistic manager of the orchestra. Bettina's role was very much focused on playing the devil's advocate and keeping a close eye on how sellable the programs would be, first to the promoters and then to their audiences. After all, this had a direct influence on the income of about 50 people. If you know this ensemble, you can imagine what wonderful program ideas were constantly flying around, because even after tailoring the ideas to their needs, the results were always exciting and innovative, ranging from baroque to contemporary.

While understanding the urge of a musician not to compromise on program ideas, a reality check is also always needed. The program you put together as a musician may make complete sense to you, but not necessarily to a "customer." Though it may seem completely obvious to you, the program might need some explaining or have a built-in compromise, i.e. have alternative works on hand that can be exchanged for some of the more challenging ideas. However, providing a guideline for why you are composing your program as you are might often result in the promoter following you on your artistic journey (as well as having an influence on the program notes).

While we advise that you take into consideration a planning committee's goals and desires, this is not to say that you should run to a promoter and tell them you can perform anything to fit their needs. If an appealing idea of theirs comes up in conversation, one can, of course, engage in this and dream up something together. However, it is not a good strategy to walk into a meeting and give them carte blanche right from the start. Rather than this making you seem flexible to their needs (and falsely reassuring you that you will be able to secure any of their concert needs that need to be filled), it weakens you and makes you come across as very unimaginative. This will hurt your reputation and your brand. Take your time when you are proposed with a different programming angle. Work on it and come back a few days later with a new proposal based on the ideas you have mutually discussed together. Don't shake your head in disbelief, we have definitely had this happen to us more than once!

You will need a few signature recital programs to offer. You will also want to show your artistic ideas for a few seasons to come, which can of course be tailored and tweaked to the needs of different promoters.

We have already spoken at length about making lists and plans in this book quite a bit, so it shouldn't be surprising that we again recommend making a plan for the next few years. What would you like to perform within the next five seasons? Which works might even be part of a much more long-term plan, in case you are just starting out? No doubt there will be works which will stick with you throughout your musical life. How you view and perform these pieces will change over the years, as will you. But keep in mind that there is always context and always a runway. For example, there are works that even if you may have studied them, they are not necessarily best for a concert stage when you are just starting out. It might not be wise to offer the "big" Beethoven or late Schubert piano sonatas, because we hardly know any promoters who would be willing to book a newly establishing player with such a heavy program. There is a time and a place for different works along your career, and giving thoughtful consideration to your programming will only help you establish your foundation and reputation.

Apart from your favorite works for your instrument, you will want to explore and come up with some original ideas. One of the obvious choices is upcoming anniversaries of composers. Most promoters will pay them tribute and program cleverly, combining their works with some aligned contemporaries, or contrasting these composers against someone very different.

Balancing the well-known with their forgotten contemporaries is also always a great idea. Have you ever checked out Étienne-Nicolas Méhul or Josef Mysliveček? The list of forgotten composers is endless.

Pianist Alexander Karpeyev (www.hellostage.com/profile/478) has chosen the forgotten Nikolai Medtner as one of his key composers and has even written a PhD about him. Alexander has built exciting piano recital programs by adding Beethoven's piano works around Medtner's compositions, and now Alexander is always remembered by Bernhard and Bettina when they come across Medtner in a different context. No doubt they are not the only ones to whom this happens.

Another idea is to tell a story with a program. One of the most beautiful and well thought out programs Bernhard and Bettina came across during their time at the Wiener Konzerthaus was Christopher Maltman and Graham Johnson's Goethe program. Poems by Johann Wolfgang von Goethe were grouped together according to the places Goethe had lived, e.g. Frankfurt, the journey to Italy, Weimar, etc. Drawing from very different composers who put these Lieder into music, they ended up with a timeline of Goethe's life, but touching upon very different styles of music. This formed a unique, colorful and fascinating recital. They chose a wonderful selection throughout time and built a most compelling program.

[10]

NEGOTIATING YOUR FEE

YOU'VE JUST HAD A great conversation with a promoter. You've firmly penciled in a date and agreed upon a program. Now they ask you for your fee. An awkward moment arises. What should you say? Or even worse – they don't raise the question themselves – so when is the right moment to approach this touchy subject?

In this chapter, we describe the all-important process of understanding how to negotiate your fee and how to take the awkwardness out of the process. After all, both sides have the same goal: they want you to perform for them and you want to be booked by them.

A key point to remember in negotiations is to truly consider the other side of the table and know what their needs and pressure points are. While it is equally critical to know your position, before you start quoting your "usual" fee, it is important to spend some time trying to understand where the promoter is coming from.

In negotiation theory, both sides will have a band in which an agreement can take place. An agreement can only be reached if both bands partially overlap in positioning.

Let's delve into the details of this theory a bit more.

For any particular concert, the promoter will have a maximum fee he is willing to pay, but he will also have an ideal fee in mind at which he would like to settle. This band between the maximum fee and the ideal fee is the promoter's agreement band.

Likewise, you as an artist or ensemble will have an ideal fee in mind that you would like to charge. Additionally, you will have a minimum fee in mind and will not perform if the offer is below this minimum. Having a minimum fee is essential in negotiating successfully. While this will mean you may say no to certain offers, it will enhance your negotiating position. We will come back to your minimum fee later in this chapter. Therefore your agreement band will range between your minimum fee and your ideal fee.

Within these two bands, there are now three theoretical possibilities:

1) THE BANDS OVERLAP PARTIALLY:

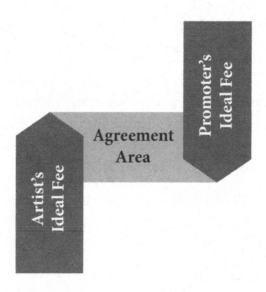

This is the best and ideal case, as when the bands overlap partially, it is easy to reach an agreement. Both sides will be happy with the outcome as it meets expectations for all parties.

2) YOUR BAND IS HIGHER THAN THE PROMOTER'S:

No Agreement

If your band is higher than the promoter's, an agreement will fail to be made. However, we would like to reiterate our position here that you never should perform for a fee under your (reasonable) minimum fee.

3) The promoter's band is higher than yours:

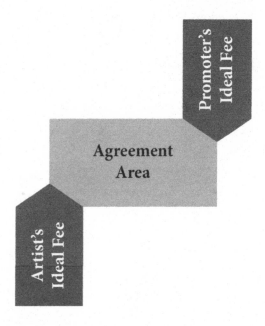

This enters dream territory! If the promoter's band is higher than yours, you might actually arrive above your ideal fee. Reaching this territory safely will depend on your sensible - and not greedy - negotiation tactics.

So then the magic question of the day becomes, "How can you know the promoter's agreement band?" Without psychic abilities, you cannot know this exact range, but the good thing is that you can estimate it fairly accurately in most cases. What you will need to know are just a few key facts:

- the seating capacity of the hall

- the average ticket price for your concert

- some background about the promoter

Much of this information is actually available online, and if not, you can ask for it. The seating capacity of the hall will tell you the maximum number of tickets that can be sold for your performance. You can often get the average ticket price directly from the promoter's website. Simply look for past concerts when artists comparable to you have performed in this same space and then pick the middle ticket price category for your estimate. These first two steps are relatively easy enough and will give you a solid foundation of data to help you analyze your situation.

Next, it will be relevant to understand the background of a promoter in order to provide context. For example, it is good to know whether the promoter is based in continental Europe or not, as most continental European promoters receive public subsidies. You should also do research and look into if there are any major sponsors. Usually a promoter's website will contain logos or background information on any public subsidies or sponsorships as part of their general public relations effort. A news search may turn up specific details and numbers as to how much of a role these sponsors and subsidies are playing in terms of the overall budget. Getting these numbers can be difficult, but any information that can be found will be helpful in providing a sense of the bigger picture from the promoter's point of view.

Generally, the level of public subsidy will be higher with promoters receiving federal subsidies. This can often mean that they also receive subsidies from their region and their city. For example, German promoters' public subsidies can range up to 80% of their annual budget, whereas for US promoters, public subsidies are negligible.

With regard to sponsorship, try to understand the size of the company by their revenue streams, and their history of support in the public arena. Often times, big companies will have a set publicized budget for philanthropy and let the world know how much they support any one endeavor. When looking at possible sponsorship deals, it will be a big difference if a venue is sponsored by an international petrol company (e.g. Chevron or Shell), or by the local petrol station around the corner.

As a rule of thumb, the maximum a promoter will be willing to pay for all artists' fees on an evening is 100% of potential ticket income. This is simply calculated by multiplying the seating capacity of the hall by the average ticket price for the evening. However, keep in mind that the promoter has also to pay for marketing, sales, taxes, tech and many other items. In some cases, he or she may even have to rent the hall too. In cases where the promoter may not own the hall, this will lower the total income even more so as he will have to pay for the venue expense.

The promoter's bandwidth now drops significantly lower, and we will need to keep in mind subsidies and sponsorships. To estimate your ideal fee, do some rough calculations. Start by thinking of how many tickets your concert will likely sell. If you have already performed at this venue before, you will have a good idea of whether you will sell out or not. The number of tickets you sell will also depend on your program. If you perform contemporary music, it is less likely to sell out than if you are playing Mozart or Beethoven. On the other hand, if you are performing contemporary music, the promoter may have some subsidies dedicated to contemporary music. Usually we have found that a promoter will most likely settle somewhere between 20% to 60% of the maximum potential ticket income for all artists' fees.

Let's run through a couple varying examples.

You are asked by a small presenter in a village to play a solo recital. The concert will take place in the local church. The church seats 100 people and tickets go for USD 15. Therefore the maximum potential ticket income for the promoter is USD 1,500 for the evening. This is probably around the maximum he is willing - and able - to pay. As this is a small promoter, he probably will depend on a lot of volunteers, will not have any public subsidies, and will need to pay a modest rental fee for the church. In this scenario, the promoter's ideal feel will probably fall between USD 300 and USD 900, knowing that the concert will not sell out and ensuring that the promoter will still be able to pay for marketing, rent, etc.

In the next example, perhaps a concert hall in Germany asks you and your colleagues to play a string quartet concert. You have regularly performed there, your concerts sell well, and you play a Haydn, Beethoven and Schubert program. The concert hall is a major city in the region and therefore clearly subsidized. The hall seats 600 people. Ticket prices for similar concerts are sold in four price categories: USD 22, USD 33, USD 40, and USD 48. The estimated average ticket price is therefore USD 35 (calculated by adding 22, 33, 40 and 48 and dividing the sum by 4). Therefore the potential maximum income for the evening is USD 21,000, representing the maximum fee the promoter is willing to pay. However, there will be numerous other expenses to take into account, so again, his ideal fee for the evening will probably be between USD 4,200 and USD 12,600.

These are just rough estimations to give you an idea of what a promoter can pay. The complexity certainly increases if an orchestra is involved or if it is an opera production. In these cases, a promoter will have to cover significantly many more costs than just your fee.

What about you? How does your fee band look like? It will depend a lot on past performances, past fees, and where you are in your career. When you are fresh out of college, your minimum fee may be a few hundred dollars. As a young but well-established artist, you can get into the thousands. Yes, superstars earn even more per performance, but don't forget that many promoters have a maximum fee they can pay. What this means is that most superstars will agree to that maximum fee as long as nobody earns more than them, or they simply do not come!

What is your ideal fee? It probably will range within two to three times your minimum fee, with your maximum fee not surpassing more than five times your minimum fee.

Having said this, we often see cases where if you've already performed in a certain place several times, you will have already established a fee history with the promoter. As you probably performed for much less in the beginning, and then both agreed again on the same (lower) fee for your second appearance, if things hopefully went well, you are now in a position to negotiate for a better fee. For your third performance, you should be able to raise your fee within the given margin, as you will have started building some fans within this promoter's audience. While the step up might not be as big as you would have wanted in the end, you can actually use this as a negotiating tactic for the following year. You can offer that if you prove yourself with this year's concert (your third appearance), you will ask for a significant level up for your fourth concert. However, you will also offer to freeze yourself at that fee for the following 2-3 seasons, so that the promoter does not feel like you are always asking for more. By offering this deal, it will reassure him that you are willing to prove yourself as a well-loved musician and also act as a fair partner in negotiations. After all, fee negotiations are always uncomfortable for promoters and musicians alike, but this offers a win-win solution and creates a lot of good will based on a record of success.

Let's go back to our earlier examples and see what you would quote. The first example was the small presenter asking for a solo recital in a local church. You are a young artist who has recently graduated, so let us set your minimum fee at USD 300, making your ideal fee USD 900. Your band therefore ranges from USD 300 to USD 900.

The promoter's band is USD 300 to USD 1,500. With a good overlap like this in both bands, an agreement should be easy to achieve.

The promoter asks you for your fee. What do you do now? Some people are good at and comfortable with negotiating, and may answer the promoter's question with a suggested fee of USD 1,000, slightly above their ideal fee from where they can be negotiated downwards. This is one possible approach that works for certain people.

However, other people, like Bernhard, hate to negotiate their fees. When Bernhard is asked for his speaker fee, he always quotes a range. In this example, he would quote USD 600 to USD 900. The outcome in both tactics will most probably be the same, but you might feel more comfortable with one negotiating tactic than the other.

Let's stick with that example for a minute and see what would happen if you were significantly more experienced and your fee band is between USD 3,000 and USD 9,000. Clearly in this instance, an agreement does not seem to be possible under these specific circumstances. Nevertheless, it is important to answer with courtesy saying that you would love to play, but that your fee is between USD 3,000 to USD 5,000. You could add that you would keep them in mind if you were in the area, to possibly add an additional concert to a tour. It actually is great to nurture relationships with smaller presenters because it can give you the chance to try out new repertoire, test artistic partners and experiment a bit. Under certain circumstances, you might be willing to lower your standard minimum fee or even waive it to go to charity.

One question we are regularly confronted with is if you should play for free. Our answer is simple and clear: No! Performing is your profession. No doctor, lawyer, consultant or waiter would work for free. There is no reason a musician should do so, even if you are passionate about what you are doing and about spreading classical music.

However, there can be times when you may receive something else in exchange for your performance besides money, so it can be beneficial to consider different options. The wonderful Schloss El-mau in Bavaria (www.schloss-elmau.de) has an eclectic chamber music program. Some of the greatest artists have been there, including Gautier Capuçon, Martin Grubinger, Ferhan & Ferzan Önder, and many others. No one gets paid any money for performing there, but they are free to develop their program and are invited to stay at this marvelous place for a few days. This is plenty of reason to come back to something like this.

Other reasons for performing without a monetary fee may include the opportunity to record or to do something for charity. Still, you should not play if there is no return for you.

In the worst cases, we have seen people wrongly take advantage of young musicians by using their passions against them to perform. Not only are they asked to play for free, but they will be asked to contribute to marketing costs or other such similar excuses. Some may do this at the last minute, saying that a sponsor did not come through, etc. There is not a single reason why a musician should actually pay to perform. Please be advised to stay away from such "opportunities".

[11]

MANAGERS AND AGENTS

THE QUESTION WE HAVE been asked the most by young musicians is how to find a manager. We have found that some young musicians graduating from music schools seem to believe that a manager will be waiting and willing to take care of their business affairs upon graduation, or that there will be several orchestral positions lined up at the ready as well. Unfortunately, this is not the case. Young musicians have to start their career on their own and will most probably need to balance a portfolio career, which includes playing in an ensemble, performing solo, and teaching.

It is important to keep in mind that approximately only 1% of all musicians worldwide actually retain management. Managers represent primarily singers, conductors, pianists, violinists and cellists, and only in very rare cases, wind players and guitarist. If you play another instrument, you have even more reason to manage your own business affairs.

Nevertheless, we find it worthwhile to delve into the issue of managers and agents. Some of you might already be working with managers, and some will do so later. Understanding early on how managers work will help you manage your own career, and if this is the path you want to take, prepare you for working with managers later on. This chapter will give you an introduction as to how agents and managers work, what you can expect from them, and what you will need to deliver.

First let's address the differences and business principles of a manager. In Europe, the roles of a manager and an agent are merged, which differs from North America. In North America, stars often have an artist manager and separate booking agents. The artist manager is responsible for setting the artist's career strategy, managing publicists, social media managers, and booking agents, as well as managing sponsorship and endorsement contracts. The booking agent is responsible for performance bookings in a certain region and maintains the calendar for given periods.

Some managers retain the right to exclusively represent an artist worldwide, which is called General Management. These managers might cooperate with local management or booking agents in certain regions to ensure that their artists are well represented in regions further away from their home office. For example, it is common that management firms based in the UK sign on as general managers and will work together with local management firms mutually chosen with the artist to ensure that the artist is well looked after in a given territory. Particularly in Italy, France, Spain, and Scandinavia, the markets work so differently that working with a local agent who has closer insight into living and working in that territory is very beneficial.

However, some artists prefer to work with several different regional managers, even on the same continent. These managers only have the right to represent an artist within the country or region assigned to them specifically, but each manager should know all about the others! For example, if you are a singer working primarily in Germany, you will have come across the fact that your colleagues may work non-exclusively with more than one agency. Although this is on the decline, it is still a common practice and can sometimes cause great confusion with promoters and opera houses. If a general management contract is offered to you, don't be afraid to put all your eggs in one basket, as this can often provide an overall smoother management experience.

An agent/manager is remunerated by a commission of 12 % to 25% of the artist's fee, depending on the country they are in, and this fee is not really negotiable. Normally, there is no fixed monthly fee, and in fact, some jurisdictions in certain countries actually forbid taking a monthly retainer. However, sometimes it makes sense to discuss a joint investment with a manager. Perhaps you would like to ensure that your digital presence is up to date or PR is taken care of in a special area, in which case a monthly payment would also be due from the artist's side.

Keeping the remuneration model for managers in mind, it is easy to roughly estimate when an artist becomes interesting for a manager. In a good agency, one manager will not manage more than five to ten artists at any given time. If they look after singers as well however, these numbers will probably go up a little. The fully loaded cost for an agency including all taxes, social benefits, work space, IT resources, travel, profit margins, etc. can easily surpass US$160,000 per year per manager. This means that the agency needs to make at least US$20,000 per year per artist represented at a base minimum. An artist will therefore need to make at least US$100,000 per year to pay an annual commission of US$20,000. With this simple calculation, it is easy to understand when it makes sense for an artist to approach a manager for representation.

Nevertheless, many managers will invest in young artists whom they find promising, even before these artists make US$100,000 per year. Managers will start working with such artists based off their confidence in them, and believing that they will easily make US$100,000 and more in a few years. However, these same managers are also sometimes faced with the tough decision of taking an artist off their roster if business does not work out over time.

What can you reasonably expect from a good manager besides finding work for you? First, a strong manager will make sure that they understand you as an artist and your artistic aspirations. They will support you in developing you along your chosen artistic path and work hard on finding the right engagements and partnerships to fit this path. The realities of business may sometimes require an artist to perform concerts or operas that are not necessarily aligned with this artistic vision, but it is a delicate balance to be worked out between the artist and manager.

A manager will also function as a trusted advisor for your career. They will sometimes be more critical than you might like, but a trusted relationship should allow for open communication, considering different viewpoints and challenging assumptions. Encouraging these open and trustful conversations are key to a successful partnership between a manager and an artist, and therefore paving the path for an artist's future career.

Another important component of the manager's role is to actively sell the artist, using their network to find the best opportunities for their artists. Unfortunately, in Bernhard's experience, this was not always the case. Often, too many managers came to the Wiener Konzerthaus with a "laundry list" of artists, proposing the firm's whole roster, without considering which artists might fit best where. A good manager maintains trustful relationships with promoters and orchestras. They will then propose artists who fit into the artistic programming strategy of a house. They will also try to understand what artistic plans are being considered early on, so that they can prepare proposals matching those. As an artist, it is good to regularly speak with your manager regarding the future artistic focuses of different houses. This way you can prepare for it, but you can also get a feeling for how strongly your manager is actually linked into different promoters and orchestras. Remember that it is also an ongoing process for them to find out information and develop deeper relationships, and they are also relying on you to tell them what you've been picking up while on the road. By working together, you can help each other further your career.

Contracts and fees are negotiated by managers as well. They finalize the contracts down to all the minute details. It makes life easier for all sides when a fee range is pre-established between the artist and the manager, to spare a new discussion every time a new proposal comes in.

Managers and artists should discuss and set out what is important with regard to contracts besides the fee range. This can include the number of days between performances, travel arrangements, practicing requirements, and many other details. As an artist, it is beneficial to think of everything that will make it easier for you to perform. You might write these points down early on, even before you have a manager. These are often simple requirements for a promoter to fulfill, but provides the necessary support so that you can perform optimally. It is self-explanatory however that such a list should not include extravaganzas.

Most management offers to take care of all travel arrangements for their artists, although some artists tend to do it themselves. Otherwise an assigned administrator will do it, who will be familiar with the artist's rehearsal time preferences on a concert day, preferred ways of traveling, and hotels. Newly signed artists are normally handed a check list of many different questions, and management will then act accordingly. This saves both sides a lot of time, energy and unnecessary correspondence.

Working with a management firm requires care to establish a trusting and professional business relationship. To ensure a successful partnership, this requires all involved parties to work closely together. Of utmost importance is the establishment of a suitable communication channel and timely responses. Email will be the most common channel, but managers are usually happy to adjust in case an artist prefers text messages, WhatsApp or similar services. Look for a channel that both sides feel comfortable using, but also take into consideration factors beyond convenience, such as being able to search for important messages from the past. Email is still significantly better for archiving and searching than various chat applications.

Critically, managers and agents will always need a timely response, which normally means within 24 to 48 hours. You should make it a part of your daily routine to work through your communication with your manager.

Artists usually only see their managers once or twice a year face-to-face. Both sides therefore need to make an effort to keep each other informed regarding new developments, any thoughts crossing one's mind, new program ideas, etc. It might be a good idea to set up a regular bi-weekly/monthly call to speak about ideas, developments and future plans. It is important to share information and ideas, seek advice and get feedback. After all, the manager–artist relationship is the most important professional partnership an artist will have.

As an artist, you will be mostly on your own traveling and giving performances, which means you will be closer to promoters than your manager will be. Therefore keep your manager informed as to how a performance went, what was discussed afterwards, and any other things you might have picked up. This enables your manager to follow up and perhaps secure a further engagement for you.

We regularly hear complaints from young as well established artists about their management companies, citing that not enough business is coming in, that their managers do not seem to be working hard enough, etc. The key to a successful partnership is patience and trust. A good manager knows his business inside and out better than any artist can. Similarly, a good artist knows exactly where his or her artistic path should take them. Both sides need to trust each other that each has their expertise and brings an important addition to the partnership. Building a career takes time. The planning cycles in classical music are long – often two to five years. An artist should not expect a full calendar only months after signing up with management. It will take a certain amount of time to build something together.

Another common complaint is that the new manager only got you re-invitations to places you have already been and did not bring any new orchestras or venues to the plate. Managers actually rely on you to bring your contacts with you so that they can work on re-invitations first. After all, the manager needs you to perform in places you already have a following so that he can invite other promoters and orchestras to experience you firsthand. Managers will also sell other artists on their roster to "your" contacts – just as they are using these other artists' contacts to sell you! Most managers keep a list of whom they spoke to and will make a note of what was discussed. You should keep such notes likewise (see the chapter about sales).

So, how do you go about finding a manager? To put it best - don't. Prepare for it and management will actually seek you out! This does not mean that you place your hands in your lap and simply wait for it to happen, but preparation is the absolute critical keyword here.

Any management company will assess your business acumen and professionalism early on, in addition to your artistic persona. Yes, they want to be taken by your musicality, your stage presence, and

your artistic message. But a manager will more often than not re-
fuse to work with an artist if he cannot trust the artist's professionalism on the business side. They will keep their ears open and listen to
what promoters, colleagues and mentors are saying about you. They
will certainly look at your digital presence and your publicity material. Having all that in order and maintaining a solid reputation with
promoters, not only on the artistic side but also on the business side,
helps.

Management will also look at your current earnings. Adding a
new artist to their existing roster is a huge investment on their part.
They have to estimate how much of their time they need to devote
to you on a monthly basis, plus get an idea of their earnings in commission for the next three to five years. Of course it won't be as much
when you are young or come with a relatively empty diary, but their
other artists will balance this out, as you will later do likewise for new
artists they take on after you.

Sometimes contact with managers can happen naturally through
your network. You might have mentors or teachers who take an interest in your professional development, who might recommend
you. Similarly, promoters as well as conductors might do so as well.
If you do feel that you are ready for a manager, you can always talk
to people in your network and seek their feedback as to whether you
seem ready for representation.

Once initial contact has been established, it will likely still be a
long process before they sign you, if at all. No doubt, you will feel the
urge to keep contacting this potential new manager, asking them to
see one of your concerts or to meet up. Please resist this urge 9 times
out of 10. Instead, send an update when there is something specific
to talk about. If you really think it is taking way too long, try asking
whoever made the introduction if they could maybe kindly find out

what is happening. There might be a million reasons that have nothing to do with you, as to why you don't have a reply yet.

We'd like to include a couple of words of caution. First, you might sometimes find so-called agents and managers approaching you and quickly asking for a monthly retainer. This fee can range from a few hundred to even thousands of dollars a month. Before you sign any such agreement, go through their roster, see if you find any friends or colleagues, and definitely speak to them. More often than not, these arrangements will not meet your expectations

Secondly, before starting to work with a manager or booking agent, always conduct your own due diligence. Ask colleagues who are currently or have been working with the manager about their feedback. Also, see how long their roster is. A long roster with just a handful of managers should ring an alarm bell. Sometimes you might want to simply add a manager to your website and hand over negotiations of contracts, etc. Agencies with long lists and few managers might just do that. But do not expect them to actively sell you nor support you strongly in your career. Remember that you want to enter a long-term partnership with a manager. Just signing up quickly with anyone does not always help your career.

We also recommend researching whether the management company you are considering is a member of an umbrella association, such as:

- the IAMA – www.iamaworld.com

- aeaa – www.aeaa.info

- der Verband der Deutschen Konzertagenturen – www.vdkd. de, or any other national ones.

You can quickly check which agencies are a part of IAMA or aeaa online at www.classicalmusicartists.com. Of course, there are also wonderful people who are not yet members of these associations, but it is usually a good indication if they are a part of a network and have been recognized.

Although we have devoted a whole chapter to working with managers and agents, ultimately they are not the key to your career. It will always be you and your musicality that are critical, but also your self-management skills. The better you can understand management skills, the more effective and efficient your future cooperation with managers and agents might be.

[12]

FANS

IMAGINE YOU HAVE A concert and nobody attends. Building your audience continuously and systematically is one of the keys to a long-term successful career. Your audience members are the ones who pay for those tickets to hear you. They are the ones who buy your recordings and they are the ones who will contribute to your crowdfunding campaign. Promoters, conductors, and managers are just the middlemen. Certainly important, but ultimately it is your audience who pays your fees in the end. Therefore you need to care about them and for them.

Pop music discovered the importance of fans early on. Great pop musicians and their managers work tirelessly to build, grow and maintain strong fan bases. A good example is the pop idol Lady Gaga. She took to social media early on and really took advantage of Facebook and Twitter to communicate directly with her fans. At the time of writing, she has over 60 million followers on Facebook and is highly active on several other social media channels. But most importantly, her fan base was strong enough to build her own social community, the Little Monsters (www.littlemonsters.com) with 1 million members. Little Monsters allows fans to interact with Lady

Gaga, but also to communicate with each other and share news, thus keeping the engine going.

For a long time, classical music has been very careful with building fan communities. Many people saw it as too commercial. Artists felt that their main duty was to perform at the highest artistic level possible, and leave the selling of tickets to promoters and the selling of albums to the record labels. But this is changing dramatically and quickly. The artistic performance is still a most critical component, but promoters are now assessing the selling potential of an artist much more often than one might think. Record labels are analyzing the fan base of artists before signing them. Having a strong fan base has become a necessity for artists, as how well an artist sells has become a significant factor, whether we like it or not. The fan base has become key to selling well.

More and more classical artists have started building up their own fan communities. A good example is the star tenor Juan Diego Flórez. While his 200,000 followers on Facebook are only a fraction of Lady Gaga's, he uses his social media presence well to not only to raise his profile, but also to get support for projects important to him. For example, Sinfónia por el Perú is a youth orchestra and music education project in his home country of Perú, which he himself supports strongly. Through his fan base, he is able to increase the support significantly and to even win corporate sponsors for it.

But where do you start with your own fans? We recommend you to think in expanding circles – starting with the people closest to you then moving outwards to more distant acquaintances.

Your family and closest friends will normally take a close interest in your career and follow it as much as possible. They will be the ones buying tickets for a performance in their area early on, to contribute to a crowdfunding campaign, and to help you as well as they can.

These are the people you can always count on to share your joys and your sorrows.

The next level circle is your network of general friends. These might be the people with whom you went to school with or whom you have traveled with. You are in regular contact with them and are always looking forward to hanging out with them.

Then there are your acquaintances. These may include people you have met occasionally or who have come backstage after a concert to congratulate you. These people take an interest in your career, but are not necessarily those you would ring up to go for a spontaneous coffee.

Among these three circles are what we call your ambassadors. These are the people who like what you are doing so much that they will happily share it with their network. You would be amazed at who these ambassadors might actually be. Surprisingly, they are not always the people closest to you. Identifying them and knowing what fascinates them about your career is important to be able to tap into when you need them. And don't worry, they *want* to support you, so you should feel free to contact them when the time is right.

It is important to be able to order your fan base into these circles, because the strength of each connection is different. With each connection, it will require a different kind of communication, frequency and contact.

Any young artist will start with a small fan base of probably no more than twenty to forty people. It takes time and effort to grow it. Perhaps no one in classical music will reach the kind of numbers Lady Gaga has, but the important goal is to nurture a loyal and growing fan base, no matter where you start. After all, Lady Gaga also started with a base of twenty to forty fans at no-name tiny music venues in New York. The crucial factor is to make sure you put in effort in building, growing and maintaining it.

Many artists are shy when it comes to connecting with their fans. Sometimes artists fear that they may lose their privacy when letting fans come too close. Other times artists feel that they do not want to bother others or may be afraid of having to communicate with strangers. But put yourself into the shoes of a fan. If a fan likes a musician, it is hard for them to passively follow an artist. Fans can actively search the internet for upcoming dates or news, but that's only if they think about doing so. Moreover, if they do search, they may be lucky if the artist's webpage is up to date so the fan can find upcoming concerts. Unfortunately, more often than not, classical musician's websites are not up to date. Sometimes it's hard for fans to follow the musicians they like because the musicians don't make it easy.

Mismanaging fans can backfire in big ways. We will share a real life example without using the names of the people involved. A friend of Bernhard's was invited to a fundraising dinner in New York for a European opera house with its music director present. This friend bought a table – to the tune of several thousands of US dollars. He had been introduced to the music director a few times beforehand and considered himself to be slightly more than an acquaintance. A year later, the music director was back in New York to conduct at the Metropolitan Opera. Bernhard's friend happened to find out about it by pure chance. Nobody had sent him an email making him aware that the maestro was in town for several weeks. Nobody had invited him to come to a performance at the Met or at least notified him about it, as complimentary tickets might not have even been necessary in this case. This is simply pure fan management, and when handled wrong, it can easily alienate people who care for your career – the ones who are willing to pay for your artistry.

Fans want to have the feeling that they know what you are up to, know where you are performing, how to get tickets, and any other relevant news. Simply put, they want to stay in the loop. They want to see that you are doing well and want to be part of your artistic journey. Today we have an array of tools, which makes it really easy and we should use them. This does not mean that we have to over-share or spam people with hundreds of emails, but a communication strategy with a certain regularity using a personal and familiar tone is relatively easy to achieve.

What are the elements one should consider?

- Provide relevant information:

    - Information about upcoming performances normally two weeks to two months in advance with links to where to purchase tickets and a few words as to why the perfor-mance is important and what to expect

    - Major news, e.g. a world premiere even a year out, an ap-pointment, an award or a prize

    - Information about broadcasts, if they can be heard online or within the country you are sending a newsletter to

    - Upcoming recordings with all details, including crowd-funding campaigns if relevant, and options to download and purchase

- Make it personal:

    - People care about you and want to have the feeling that they are in contact with you directly. They know that you cannot write to everyone personally, but a personal note or a clever use of visuals helps to give it a personal touch.

- Violinist Hillary Hahn found a funny way of bridging her need for privacy, while still maintaining communication with a personal touch. In her Twitter account – www.twitter.com/violincase – with over 70,000 followers, she lets her violin case speak for her.

- Nevertheless, in the digital language of the 21st century, the direct-to-fan experience has established itself strongly. It is this personal, direct communication that helps fans develop an emotional, loyal bond.

• Allow for interaction whenever possible:

- Communication is a two-way street. Your fans not only want to receive up-to-date information about your career, but also want to interact with you from time to time. Channeling interaction and allowing it can make your fan base significantly stronger. There are many ways to do that – from personal meetings to online sessions, live video feeds, and asking fans for their opinions online.

So what are the tools one can use to manage one's fan base? Luckily there are a growing number of software and online tools available, making it so much easier than the days of old when Bernhard started his singing career and he had to print newsletters, put them in an envelope, address them, buy stamps and send them off by mail. Yes by mail, not email.

It all starts with a database. Your database should organize and keep track of all names, email addresses, and any additional information you gather about your fans. This can be done in an Excel spreadsheet, using database software, or utilizing different online tools. However, make sure that all the data is handled with only commonly used software or online tools. One of the most important requirements is the ability to download your database into a commonly used format. Facebook, Twitter and other social media platforms do not enable you to do that. Furthermore, you need to be able to add custom fields so that you can sort and segment your database.

The minimum information you should collect about your fans includes:

- Their name

- Their partner's name

- Their main city

- Their email address

- Where and when you met them first

- Which circle they belong to and if you see them a potential ambassador

- Any further information on their musical tastes from favorite composers to instruments to genres

A good way to start is to simply collect business cards after concerts and at other opportunities. There is even good software out there which allows you to scan business cards with your smartphone so that you don't have to enter all the details by hand. Professional sales people often jot down a few notes on the backs of business cards to remember pertinent information, such as the above details, to be entered into their databases later. Making this a habit can help you build strong connections.

Imagine that you are playing your first concert in Salzburg and that you had met someone from Salzburg a year prior in London. Dropping this person a short email saying that you will be performing in Salzburg and how nice it was to have met a year ago in London will make most people an engaged fan of yours. They will likely help you in Salzburg if needed, and would probably be happy to introduce you to their friends.

Another good tip, especially if you are out there after your recital selling your CDs in the foyer, is to simply put out a piece of paper and a pen for people to sign up for your mailing list. Some artists even use an iPad in these situations and add people directly to their mailing list, which then goes straight into their database.

One caveat on the database: privacy and data protection is important and has been legally imposed in many jurisdictions. Your database is a valuable asset where people have given you permission to collect their address information, as they have handed you their business card. You never should hand that database or parts of it over to someone else. If a promoter asks you, you can offer to send an email to the relevant addresses yourself. But you should not – and are often not allowed to – give database entries you have collected on your own.

Although we are living in a digital age, meeting people in person is still so much stronger. Making time to meet fans after a concert, at events, or on special occasions is important. Some of the biggest stars even make sure to see their strongest supporters for coffee or lunch in the respective cities they are performing at.

Sometimes you might ask one of your closer friends or supporters if you could play a house concert at their place for their friends. This is a great opportunity to actually test out new repertoire or just to play a program once more in front of an audience before going onto a bigger stage. For your inner circle of fans, it will be a unique opportunity to come closer to you, feel special, and build an emotional bond.

Before going into the various electronic tools available, it is important to point out that there are many means of communicating directly with fans. A short email, even better a personal card, or a phone call on the rare occasion, can go a long way. One pianist we know likes the personal touch of handwritten notes. Knowing that he is traveling so much, he simply photographs them or scans them and attaches them to emails. It stands out as a very personal way of communicating in the 21st century.

The easiest way to relay information and a key tool is the newsletter. This can cover all layers of fans and supporters. Newsletters need to be concise, informative, relevant and regular. Sending a newsletter every one to three months has proven to be a good pattern. Keep in mind that most emails are now read on a mobile device. According to Litmus' "Email Analytics" (March 2016), 55% of emails are now read on a smartphone. And that percentage is only growing.

WHAT SHOULD BE INCLUDED IN A NEWSLETTER?

- A short personal introductory paragraph/message from you

- A list of upcoming concerts with links to purchase tickets

- Any new news

- Links to download or stream your music

- Links to your social media channels and to your website

A good newsletter should have good visuals - not too many, but a few to make it easy to read.

If you have a good database, you can even start sending newsletters to specific segments of your fan base. This increases the reading rate of your newsletters significantly. For example, you might send a very short newsletter only to the fans in the town where you are performing next. Segmenting becomes an art in marketing, but can make messages much better received.

There are several online tools for sending email newsletters, and it is advisable to use their services to ensure that your email is delivered to the recipient's address and not land in their spam folder.

One of the most widely used tools is Mailchimp (www.mailchimp.com). It allows you create newsletters in various formats for all devices. It also enables you to have a list and segment it. You can add a sign-up form for your Mailchimp newsletter on your Facebook page and your webpage.

HELLO STAGE (www.hellostage.com) has developed an automatic monthly newsletter for its members. Fans can register on the page of the musician and/or ensemble, and they will receive a monthly newsletter with upcoming performances and news. As a musician, you only need to keep your HELLO STAGE page up-to-date and everything else happens automatically, making it highly convenient.

Social media certainly plays an important role in fan management, which we discuss in further detail in the chapter SOCIAL MEDIA STRATEGY. What we will say here is that social media allows you to share background stories and more frequent information. It is pull marketing as we discussed before, where fans need to interact on social media with you in order to receive information. A newsletter falls under push marketing, landing in their inbox until they unsubscribe. A thoughtful strategy regarding when to use social media (pull) versus when to use newsletters (push) is useful in increasing your fan engagement.

A few last words: building a fan base takes time and has a lot to do with trust. People will be more likely to trust you if you keep your interactions personal. Authenticity matters. Secondly, never forget to put yourself in the shoes of your fans. How often have you, as a fan, heard from artists you like informing you about their next concerts?

How often have you actually done this for your fans? Remember that people who like you want to hear from you and see you perform.

[13]

CROWDFUNDING

YOUR FANS WILL NOT only build the core of your loyal audience, but also for any of your crowdfunding activities. Crowdfunding is a new way to finance projects and ideas enabled by the internet. It might be an interesting alternative in financing your next project. The principle behind crowd funding is to motivate lots of people to give incremental amounts of money to a project, as opposed to a sponsorship, where you would ask for a lump sum of money from one or two persons or companies.

Crowdfunding has been enabled by the internet and through simple communications via online platforms, which we will discuss later in this chapter. It allows you to tap directly into your network of friends and acquaintances to support your project.

You can crowdfund any project. The Pebble Watch, a smart watch, raised over US$20M from 78,000 backers on one of the crowdfunding platforms and set the record there. HELLO STAGE has been involved in many crowdfunding projects, most of which were CD projects raising around US$10,000.

When should you consider crowdfunding? Crowdfunding is a great tool to finance a clearly defined project with a well-defined outcome and a specific timeline. We recommend that crowdfunding be used for projects with a physical product, e.g. a CD, because people tend to respond to tangible products. However, we have seen successful crowdfunding projects for commissioning new music and other projects as well. Again, as long as the project is well-defined and therefore easily understood, crowdfunding can often provide the right kind of financing.

An important aspect of crowdfunding is to spin the communication right. You are not begging or asking for money. You are offering people the opportunity to become part of a fascinating story. With physical products, this can even be seen as a pre-sales tool. When raising money for CDs, people can pay now via crowdfunding and will later receive a CD as a so-called perk. You would be surprised by how much people love to be involved in interesting projects. Give them a chance to be part of your work!

In the following, you will find explanations regarding each step you need to think of when doing a crowdfunding campaign. An important piece of advice – crowdfunding is a great tool to finance your project, but is also an immense amount of work. Make time for it in your daily schedule.

THE PROJECT

You are completely free in the definition of your project. There are no limits to your creativity, you just need to make sure that you can communicate it clearly and easily so that everyone understands it quickly. A project needs to be well defined, have a clear outcome, and a reasonable timeline. Projects can be the making of a CD, a book, a commission for new music, the prototyping of a new instrument, or even buying an instrument for you.

Projects that have a physical product generally seem to do better than others. Raising money for a CD or a book will be easier because you are effectively preselling the product. For people to support the commissioning of a new work, they need to buy into the idea, which is trickier, but has been done as well.

For example, the Piano Duo Ferhan and Ferzan Önder (www.hellostage.com/ferhanferzan) successfully raised EUR 18,205 from only 44 backers in 2015 for a project called "Anonymous Was a Woman" (www.wemakeit.com/projects/anonymous-was-a-woman). They commissioned six female composers to write new pieces for a piano duo. The perks people chose included a private concert and being named on all the scores.

Test your project definition with friends. If they understand your project from your short description within three sentences, you are good to go. If they have questions after that, refine your project definition.

When describing your project on any of the crowdfunding platforms, you will need to include your intents on what will be done with the money. You do not need to include a detailed budget, but people will want to know roughly what their money is used for.

Good crowdfunding platforms will also ask you to describe potential risks and challenges, which could make the project a failure or jeopardize the timeline. It is important that you think about these issues as well – not only because the platform asks you for it, but also to manage your project well. You might reach out to people who have done similar projects and ask them what challenges they encountered. Often the promised timing in crowdfunding projects is too ambitious.

TIMELINE

A crowdfunding project will easily take up a whole year of work. The timeline can be divided into three phases:

- Preparation

- Campaign

- Fulfillment

PREPARATION

During the preparation period, you will need to define the project clearly, develop a communication plan, decide on a platform to use, get your budget together, and start building your network. This phase easily takes three months.

Starting to build your network early on is an especially crucial success factor. You need to have a mailing list of people who know you and who have heard you. Start asking people you meet for their email addresses and collect them systematically. Use tools described in the chapters about your DIGITAL PRESENCE and your FANS. Tell people at concerts that you are planning to record an album and ask them for their email addresses so that you can keep them informed.

A good example of using this preparation time successfully to build interest in a campaign comes from a very different industry. Daniela Castellanos started a campaign to sell backpacks made by indigenous Colombian women. She started communicating about it around four to six months before she actually started the campaign, and quickly reached 100% of her goal within the first initial days of her campaign (www.kickstarter.com/projects/castellano/wayuu-backpack-support-colombian-hand-craftsmanshi). Because she had built the runway before releasing her campaign, she primed her project for success.

CAMPAIGN

The campaign itself will require a lot of time from you every day. Campaigns run between 30 and 45 days, which gives you enough time to communicate about it within your network and reach out to people, but not to overuse your contacts.

HELLO STAGE members have often set aside two hours every day to work on their campaigns. In that time, they reached out to people, sent emails, made social media posts, and thanked people who contributed. Personally thanking people early on is important. You might end up reaching out to people to top up their contributions towards the end of the campaign, so you will want to keep them informed and close.

You can break the campaign into three phases – the start, middle and finish. Normally contributions to your campaign happen in the very first days, in the middle if you communicate correctly, and towards the end to ensure that you reach your goal. Keep these phases in mind for your communication, but also to manage your own expectations. There will be days between the start and the middle, as well as between the middle and the finish, where you will not receive any contributions. Don't worry about it, but keep doing what you are doing.

The start of a campaign should always be strong, so make sure that you have a few good friends and family members lined up who will contribute in the first few hours of the campaign. This gives the campaign movement and something positive to communicate about to the rest of your potential donors.

Many people add additional perks, sometimes really fun ones, in the middle of the campaign. This helps in the communication aspect and will generate more attraction and interest in your campaign.

The last few days of a campaign are really important. Often people raise 50% of the overall budget in the last few days. Ask the people who have already contributed for help, not only in topping up their contribution, but also to tell their friends about your great campaign and help spread the word. This will enlarge the reach of your campaign and help its ultimate success.

FULFILLMENT

Congratulations if you raised all the money you wanted! Unfortunately, the work is not over yet. You will be excited to realize your project, which is great, but your backers will be waiting to hear about the project and receive the perks you promised them. Therefore you will need to continue to communicate with them. They want to feel as if they are part of the project, so let them! Remember also that this will not be the last campaign, and that at some point, you will reach out to them again. The closer they feel to you, the better.

If your project is delayed for whatever reason and you cannot send out the promised perks, make sure you communicate about it. People normally don't have a problem with it as long as they know what is happening.

When sending out perks, add a handwritten card and perhaps some nice promotional material like stickers or postcards. A handwritten card goes a long way in today's digital world. Remember, even Apple still packages its sticker into all their shippings. Your backers not only gave you money, they are now a part of your project. Acknowledge that and use it for the success of this and future projects.

One question remains on when is a good time to run a crowdfunding campaign. We recommend staying away from holiday periods – December and January, as well as July and August. It is harder to reach people during those time periods and they tend to spend less on ancillary expenditures.

COMMUNICATION

The key to any successful crowdfunding campaign is communication. If you do not have a good email list or a strong social media presence, crowdfunding might not be the right answer for you.

Your communication first starts out with a large enough pool you can actually communicate with. Ideally, many of the people you know become multipliers for your campaign.

Communications about your crowdfunding project should be, as with any communication, short and to the point. People do not read more than what fits on their screen. An email with three paragraphs of five sentences each is as long as it should get. Be clear in asking what you want from people. This should be as clear as: "Please go to [insert URL of your crowdfunding project] and become part of my project now." Remember that you may be communicating with many people whose first language is different from yours.

Communication about the project itself should start early on – much earlier than your actual campaign. This gives people the feeling that they are to be part of the project, rather than being asked to donate money.

At the actual start of your campaign, you should send out an email newsletter widely informing people about your project and asking them to participate and to share the project. At the same time, make sure that you are sharing the project via your own social media channels. If you have identified friends beforehand who are excited about the project, ask them to share it via their social media channels as well.

Social media is a good way to keep people informed on a daily basis about your project. Emails should not be sent out that often, rather only three to four times over the course of a campaign. Tell them about new perks, about people who have contributed, behind the scenes stories of your project, and more. Good communication is not about always asking for money, but in making people feel part of the project itself. The more you can build an emotional and personal connection, the stronger the support will be.

Make sure you thank people personally in an email for their contribution within a day of them signing up for the project. This builds trust and shows that you are dedicated to the project.

Another email during the middle of the campaign can be helpful. Here you should segment your mailing list between people who have already contributed and people who have not. People who have contributed will want to know relevant news on where you are in reaching your goal, hear another thank you, and perhaps get some funny background stories. For people who have not yet contributed, express how excited you are to have already reached X% of your goal and about the great feedback you have gotten so far. Make them want to be part of it and do ask them clearly to join in.

In the lead up to the final days before the end of the campaign is another time to reach out to your network. Thank people who have contributed thus far and ask them to top up their contribution so the project can reach its target. Give people who have not contributed as of yet one last chance to become part of your amazing project.

Communication does not stop after you have successfully raised the money. Keep people informed regularly. You can include the news in your regular newsletter and post news on social media.

BUDGET

Before getting started on numbers, there are two different kinds of crowdfunding options: a fixed goal or a flexible goal. Most crowdfunding platforms only use fixed goals. This means that you set a specific amount of money you want to raise and that you must raise that amount in order to receive the contributions. If you do not hit the goal, the money will be returned to the backers. However, you can set this limit lower and always have the opportunity to overachieve your goal like many projects do.

When deciding upon a flexible goal, you do not need to reach any specific number. You will receive all the money contributors put towards the project. The only big platform to offer this option of flexible goals is Indiegogo (www.indiegogo.com).

When drawing up a budget, it is important to keep these two different options in mind. If you go for a fixed goal, you need to make sure that you create a minimum budget that will allow you to realize your project, but still keep the money needed as low as possible. There is no harm in overachieving your fundraising goal. All platforms allow you to receive more money than your initial goal. You even might add another part of your story to a crowdfunding project. Overreaching your goal might, for example, allow you to include a video shooting for your new album in the project.

The good thing about fixed goal campaigns is that you can always add stretch goals. This means that you can add into your project description the things that you would do if you overachieve your goal. This provides backers with an illumination of where their money goes when you overreach your goal.

For example, let's say you are raising money for a CD and you use a platform with fixed goals. You will include all recording and production costs in the minimum budget, but a video trailer or market-ing material can be added as stretch goals in the project description.

Communicate openly, transparently, and honestly about your budget. This builds trust with your backers. They will see that you have thought through everything carefully. Give them an idea of three to five main expenditure items which are included in your project. This will require you to go out and get quotes for what you need before you can start your campaign.

An important point to include is the platform fees when drawing up your budget. Most crowdfunding platforms take 5% of all money raised for any given project, plus an additional 3% to 5% for payment processing. This means that you will need to add roughly 10% to your overall budget to cover all platform related fees.

You will also need to include the actual costs of any perks you of-fer. A lot of the perks you offer will be something you do. If you are running a campaign for your album and want to ship physical CDs, you will need to include the actual cost of the CD, packaging, post-age, etc.

You are well advised to clarify your tax situation with your tax advisor before starting your campaign. Many tax advisors are not yet familiar with crowdfunding, and neither are most tax authorities. You need to ensure that the crowdfunding campaign is seen as the fi-nancing part of a project from a tax perspective - and not as personal income. This means that you can offset all related costs against mon-ey received, and should only be taxed on any profits which might re-main. This requires a proper accounting on your side to ensure that all related costs are captured correctly.

Another interesting aspect when thinking of your budget is to know that there might be sponsorship or matching opportunities for your project. WeMakeIt in Austria collaborates regularly with

Bank Austria. Bank Austria will give 1/3 of the goal to a project, if the project was already able to raise the first 1/3 by itself. You might ask wealthy individuals or companies you know to match any funding you can raise on your own. It is a simple ask, as you are already seen being quick on your feet and finding ways to finance your project. Match funding is especially popular in Anglo-Saxon countries.

THE CROWD

The most critical factor in any crowdfunding campaign is the crowd itself. It is entirely up to you to build up your own crowd. Without a following, crowdfunding platforms will almost never be of help, even if it is said otherwise.

Your crowd starts with the people closest to you – your family and your closest friends. Don't be afraid to talk to them about your project early on. Make them a part of your project by asking for their opinion and feedback, and incorporate their ideas wherever useful. The more they feel a part of it, the more they will feel compelled to not only support you directly, but to also reach out to their friends and acquaintances. They will become the best ambassadors for your project.

People who have heard you in concert will be interested in following your path. Enable them to do so. Collect their email addresses, inform them about your project early on in personal conversations, at dinners, and even from the stage if the promoter agrees. The clearer your message is and the more they feel your passion for the project, the better.

Harpist Coline-Marie Orliac (www.hellostage.com/Coline-Marie-Orliac) had a crazy idea to record pieces by Frederic Chopin on the harp. For her, it was simply about this great music she wanted to play. She felt left out that Chopin wrote so much for the piano, but nothing for the harp. Because of her feelings, she decided to record an album with works by Frederic Chopin played only on the harp. She created a crowdfunding campaign for her project and raised US$13,000, overachieving her goal by 26%! (www.kickstarter.com/projects/522921495/harpistically-yours-chopin)

An issue that gets raised sometimes is how often you actually can go to your network to raise money. This is a tricky question, and yes, your crowd might get tired of projects. Considering your side of the equation, how often do you come up with fascinating new projects worth a crowdfunding campaign? Definitely not more than once a year. Probably more like every two to three years. This is a suitable break for your crowd, although it is key to keep them informed and give them the feeling that they are a part of your artistic journey.

YOUR STORY

Every platform will ask you to provide your story for your project. The description of the projects is quite important. Make the project description relevant and interesting, especially for people who normally do not have anything to do with classical music.

Your story starts with you. Tell people who you are, what makes you tick, and how you arrived to the proposed project. They want to get to know you and your background. Don't copy your biography, but write specifically to how you got on the path to your project. Again, keep it short and to the point.

A valuable factor in your story is your passion for the project. How did you come up with it? Why is it so significant to you? We described before how harpist Coline-Marie Orliac was so fascinated by Chopin's music that she wanted to play it on her instrument, the harp. This is a credible and fascinating story people like to be involved in.

Like all modern communication, crowdfunding platforms also rely heavily on visuals. It starts with a short video. This does not need to be professionally done, but should look nice and bring people closer to you. Give people a brief summary of your project and why you are so moved by it. Videos should be much shorter than you might think – one minute is great, but three is the absolute maximum.

Your story should include photos and pictures. These should be relevant to the project itself and not just professional shots of you. Coline-Marie Orliac included a private photo of hers in front of a Chopin statue.

Testimonials can add credibility to your story. If you get a good testimonial from a well-known musician who really knows you, great. For our campaign for this book, we asked young musicians for their testimonial, as this seemed to be most relevant to our story. You can think creatively about which testimonials best support your story.

PERKS

A fun part of all crowdfunding campaigns are the perks. These are rewards people receive in exchange for contributing to your campaign.

You should offer a range of different perks at different price levels. We recommend creating at least five different perks, if not more. It is good to start at a very low level, often with US$1-5. The majority of people will be attracted by perks between US$20-50, but it is important that you include perks at several higher levels, often going into the thousands of dollars. Ensure that you have the price ranges well distributed so that there is no large gap e.g. between US$50 and US$2,000.

You actually do not need to add all the perks at the beginning of your campaign. It is often fun to add some in over the course of the campaign, especially if you can use the additions as reasons for communication.

You can think in four different categories of perks and actually mix them in any way you want:

- Digital perks

- The product itself

- Product additions

- Fun perks

Digital perks can be a simple message on the Facebook page of a backer. They can also be the digital download of one track of your CD, or the pdf file of one chapter of your book. As digital perks are only delivered digitally, there are no shipping costs involved and are easy to replicate for you. It's a great perk for a low price but with high volume.

The product itself depends on your project. It can be a CD, a book, or another physical product. If your project involves an intangible product like a new piece of music, think of something tangible you can send out, such as the score or parts of the score. People like to receive something. When thinking about products, make sure that you can actually ship them. Books, CDs, scores, etc. are all easy. A big sculpture or painting might become really difficult. Many crowd-funding platforms allow you to add shipping cost to a perk. Research shipping costs beforehand so that they do not go towards your overall budget.

There are many ways to enhance your product. This starts with signing your CD or book, to adding special packaging. Again, make it personal. A beautiful example is Maria Weiss' Favola in Musica (www.hellostage.com/mariaweiss). This is a CD with early and contemporary music recorded in a cold mountain church in Austria. Maria loves beautiful things and her Instagram account is full of amazing photos from her kitchen table (www.instagram.com/earlymusic. bird). In her crowdfunding campaign, as well as still offered in her online shop, she offered the CD handwrapped by her - an art in itself (www.favolainmusica.com/shop/cd-3/2975).

It is always great to add fun perks to your campaign. Think about what makes you special beyond your music. You might love books, a special wine, hiking or whatever. Think of perks that you can offer around this other passion. Bernhard is an espresso fanatic. As a part of the crowdfunding campaign for this book, he offered to take backers to his favorite coffee shops in specific cities. The New Piano Trio (www.hellostage.com/New-Piano-Trio) offered backers to go hiking with them in Switzerland (www.wemakeit.com/projects/new-piano-trio).

The ultimate perk is always having you perform a private concert. More often than not, people actually like the idea of having a musician perform in their home. They are even willing to pay for all extra costs involved from your travel to renting a piano. However, make sure that you are transparent about the additional costs involved and set the price high, as this truly is a special perk.

PLATFORMS

With a growing number of crowdfunding platforms out there, choosing the right one is not easy. Keep in mind that the size of the platform itself is less relevant. Choosing one platform over another will not materially help you in raising more money for your project. Comparing costs is also not really essential, as they tend to be pretty similar.

The most critical component to consider is the payment provider. This is the partner of the platform that actually facilitates the credit card payments of your backers. You would be surprised at how much more difficult this is than you might think, most especially because you might have backers from many different countries around the world. The platforms will not necessarily tell you whom they are using, and even if so, it might not mean much to you. We will break it down below to help you navigate the different options.

When choosing your crowdfunding platform, one factor to consider is its brand name and therefore the trust people have in it. If most of your backers are locally in and around your country, and using a platform supported by local banks, this is probably a good choice. However, if your backers are from all over the world, you should go for one of the international brand names. Most projects HELLO STAGE has been involved in included backers from over 20 countries. Only an international platform can handle that.

Kickstarter (www.kickstarter.com) is a clear market leader. It has a global reach and one of the best brand names for crowdfunding. Its projects are very diverse from the cited Pebble Smart Watch to books and arts projects. Payments are processed via Amazon Payments, ensuring that most people around the world can pay easily. Projects need to hit their goal mark in order for you to receive the money.

Indiegogo (www.indiegogo.com) offers flexible goals, allowing you to receive all the money contributed, even if you did not hit your goal. While it uses PayPal as a payment provider, there have been known to be issues with it. This means that backers were ultimately not able to contribute to a project. We believe these issues will be solved over time, but it is worth considering this matter and checking it out before committing your project to Indiegogo.

A smaller, but recommended platform is wemakeit (www.wemakeit.com). Based in Switzerland, they not only offer multi-language support, but also provide you with individual feedback on your campaign. It has the personal touch that bigger platforms are missing. Wemakeit also works with corporate partners, adding different funding opportunities for your project.

You will find updates on the various crowdfunding platforms on our website (www.be-your-own-manager.com). Do also let us know of your experiences so that we can share up-to-date information within our classical music community.

We highly encourage you to try out crowdfunding. It is an interesting tool and not only helps you finance your artistic projects, but also helps build a strong fan base which is important for your future career.

[14]

YOUR FIRST RECORDING

MANY YOUNG MUSICIANS USE crowdfunding to finance their first recording. It is a wonderful tool to cover most of the often really high costs of creating your first album. But how do you actually start with your first recording project?

An album serves as a business card for musicians. In the traditional world of classical music, many people still want to listen to a physical CD instead of downloading an online digital file. Therefore many musicians are faced with the task of producing a CD for the first time. In this chapter we will explain the various issues to consider when working on your first recording and suggestions as to how to go about it.

Any album project will always start with the question of repertoire. What should you actually record? Before we answer that question, it is necessary to first take a step back and think about what the purpose of the recording is. You should not expect your first recording to hit the Billboards or be a sales hit. It should actually be geared much more towards introducing yourself to orchestras, promoters, and managers. You will want to keep this in mind when thinking about the repertoire to record.

The average CD has between 50 to 70 minutes to fill. Since your first recording will function as your calling card to get you concerts, it should show you at your absolute best and contain a range of different pieces. So think about what kind of music and repertoire you stand for, then select the best pieces from that. Make sure that the album has a lot of variety, with virtuoso pieces as well as slower ones, classical and some pieces closer to contemporary music. We would be slightly hesitant to record some of the great masterpieces such as the Goldberg Variations or some of the well-known Beethoven Sonatas. Look for repertoire that fits you and where the pieces are not too long. You might combine one piece that runs 10 to 12 minutes with a few shorter ones of 3 to 5 minutes in length.

Having said that, sometimes there are artists who take a risk because they feel so moved to play a certain masterpiece. American pianist Simone Dinnerstein (www.hellostage.com/Simone-Dinnerstein) was so fascinated by Johann Sebastian Bach's Goldberg Variations that she simply had to record them. She shopped the recording around and got the (no longer existing) label Telarc to publish it. It was her breakthrough. Bernhard remembers well when Simone's manager introduced her in a meeting in Vienna. She left the Goldberg Variation recording behind. Bernhard, a Bach lover, did not want to touch it, surprised that an unknown pianist would dare to record such a masterpiece. One day he listened to it, quite by accident, having picked up the CD from a pile of many. He was so intrigued by the interpretation that he stopped working and started to listen carefully. He ended up inviting Simone Dinnerstein, now a Sony Artist, to perform at the Wiener Konzerthaus several times.

Another exception to the rule is the cellist Marianne Dumas (www.hellostage.com/marianne-dumas) who is discovering breakthroughs in the art of the baroque cello, best demonstrated with Johann Sebastian Bach's 6 Cello Suites. Marianne actually embarked on recording these known masterpieces herself, but Ton Koopman and YoYo Ma have already embraced her. The results of her risk-taking will soon be revealed, but we believe that this recording will be a huge success as well.

Another question related to repertoire is whether to record on your own or with partners. As a singer, you normally record with a pianist. But should you record a solo repertoire as a cellist, or work with a pianist, or record with a string ensemble? We normally recommend recording with at least piano accompaniment. It offers more variety and is therefore more interesting to listen to. If you are pushing a chamber music career, you should obviously consider recording with an ensemble. However, if you are focusing on a solo career, a recital style recording might be more right for you. There are, however, other combinations you might want to think about. Harp and flute is a very well-known combo. Star Flutist Jasmine Choi (www. hellostage.com/jasmine-choi) dared to do an early recording with a jazz trio, showing off her jazzier side. She recorded Claude Bolling's Suite for Flute and Jazz Trio for Sony Classical. When considering recording with partners, think about musicians you respect, ones you work well with, and ones whom you could potentially play concerts with as well. The recording should be just one step of a musical partnership.

Some musicians ask their teachers or mentors to record with them. This can be a good opportunity if you can control the recording and it is seen as your recording. However, a bigger name might push you aside in the eyes of a promoter, even if it was not intended that way. Yet it can also give you more clout at the same time, so see how you feel about the perceived risks and balances.

Before going into the studio, you should run through the repertoire you have decided upon in several concerts. It is unimportant whether you play it in big venues or across several house concerts.

Just perform it in front of an audience and get used to playing it. Ideally you will have performed it at least five times before going into the studio. This is not only true for first recordings, but very much common practice for any good recording. The Deutsche Kammerphilharmonie Bremen played all of the Beethoven Symphonies with Paavo Järvi on several tours before going into the studio to record their prize-winning repertoire.

When it is time to select a studio, ask around for recommendations. There are many good choice in lots of cities, but you should select one specializing in classical music and one that is experienced in working with young musicians. Ideally you will find a team composed of a producer and a sound engineer. Another approach is to search for a freelance producer who will then choose the studio and sound engineer for you. These producers are often familiar with various studios across the world, as they will generally have worked in a bunch of them already and be familiar with their inner workings.

Get to know the producer and/or the sound engineer you will be working with. It is important that you feel truly comfortable with them, as their input on your recordings can be massive. They will be the ones who will tell you to re-record a passage, make acoustic suggestions, and serve, in general, as your second set of ears. Their experience and your comfort levels in getting their feedback is essential for a good time in the studio.

A well-prepared solo or chamber music recording will take between three to five studio days. These are normally done on consecutive days, and you will want to plan these days well. First of all, make sure that you are not only fully rehearsed and prepared, but also that you are wholly rested and focused. You should be able to channel your full energies on your recording and focus on it completely. Make sure to sleep enough on the days before and during the recording days, and cancel any other appointments and meetings. Switch on an autoresponder in your email inbox to let people know you will not respond for the next few days.

Make a schedule for the recording days well in advance and review it in advance with the producer, sound engineer and your pianist if applicable. It is good to start with shorter pieces that you feel very comfortable and happy with. Record them first so that you have a good start. However, do not leave the longest and most difficult pieces to the end. Rather, do them on the second day after you've had a chance to warm up with your easier pieces. Also, don't jampack your recording schedule all the way up until the last minute. Leave ample time for repeats and time to listen to the recordings. If a day goes well, stop recording earlier and get some rest, then start the next day refreshed. Also plan for breaks – all of you will need them. If you are lucky enough to record with an orchestra, find out what time their rules demand a break so that you can work your schedule around this.

Besides going into a studio, there is always the option of live recordings. You might get lucky if one of your concerts is recorded by a radio station. The only issue with live recordings is that you often cannot correct any mistakes, but you might very well be able to put together a good album from various live recordings. Just make sure that you have the rights to use live recordings. Sometimes they can be a little hard to get so raise the issue early on when negotiating the concert. In case the recording is only for your personal archive or to be used as a marketing CD that is not publicly sold, it will probably be much easier to get the rights. If you are already quite sure that you would like to use the live recording in advance, you can ask the broadcasting station during negotiations if they would allow for a little patch session after the recital. This way you can easily correct the few bits and pieces that need fixing that you (or they) might realize during the actual performance. Always make sure this is ok for both the promoter and the hall, as staff will need to stay overtime for you in this case.

No album is ever done after the recording. The real and often tedious work only starts there. It then becomes all about the mixing and mastering. Most of this work will be done by the producer/sound engineer, but you will still need to listen to the tapes regularly in order to provide input and suggestions. You should always go through all the tapes with your scores in your hand and check that everything is correct. Bars can go missing or be repeated. We recommend listening to the tapes in the studio with the engineers. The sound quality there is significantly better and you will be able to hear nuances that you won't hear on your speakers or headphones at home. In case you have a really busy schedule, make sure you have the best headphones possible and listen to the tapes on long journeys.

When all this is done, you will now have the master tape in your hand. Actually, it is mostly not a tape anymore these days, but a digital file. The next step then focuses on manufacturing the CD and its subsequent distribution.

Ideally one of the well-known labels would be interested in publishing your recording. This can be awesome, but look at the terms very, very carefully. Some labels ask a lot of money from the artist for marketing, expenses, and etc., but keep most of the sales receipts. They also might ask for a percentage from your live performing fees, arguing that the album is a good marketing tool for getting bookings. Nevertheless, it can be worthwhile to have a brand name on your album. It makes your album more interesting for promoters, so you should definitely consider it, but just carefully.

Another option is to go the self-publishing route. There are various labels that offer this option. Normally you will have to pay for the manufacturing costs, but you also get to keep most of the sales revenues. These labels also give you access to publish your album on various digital channels that mostly do not accept albums from individual artists. When looking for distribution partners, make sure that they can provide you with a label code. Unfortunately the music industry still does not have a universal label code comparable to the ISBN for books. However, there are codes which will need to be on your CD and will help it get sold on various channels. Furthermore, your distribution partner should have contracts with at least one royalty collecting society to ensure that you get paid whenever your CD is played on the radio.

Another benefit of working with an established partner is clarifying any issues centered around copyrights. Generally speaking, though with many national differences, works by composers who have been dead for over 70 years are considered to be in the public domain. When something is in the public domain, you can record them for free. Sometimes however, the scores of these pieces are edited by a publishing company, which then carries copyrights. Before publishing your CD and making it available for general purchase, clarify the rights issues, either with your label partner or with a good copyright lawyer.

With self-publishing, you can have significantly more freedom in the artwork of your CD as well as the booklet. When considering the artwork, re-read the chapter PHOTOS AND VIDEOS, and consider that the artwork for your album will not only appear on the cover of your CD, but also as an icon on iTunes, Spotify, etc. This can prove to be quite a challenge for any graphic designer. Remember that these icons can be very small, so you will want to think of what they may look like in a tiny format.

A booklet should be part of every CD, and should be written at least in English. Many booklets are often written in several languages to appeal to local markets. The booklet should include a bio of all the artists involved, a short text about the concept of the recording, and some text on the music itself. It is also the best place to thank all your supporters and the people worked with you on the recording, from any donors to the producer, sound engineers and graphic designers.

When it comes to selling, you will always be the best salesperson for your album. You would be astonished by how many people like to buy a CD after a concert. Trombonist Peter Steiner (www.hellostage.com/peter-steiner) went on a US promotion tour for his album "UNITED" in January and February of 2017 and quickly sold 500 CDs. Violinist Viktoria Mullova always brings CDs to her concerts and asks someone from the promoter staff to sell them after the concert for her. Don't be shy and get out there! People love to get your CD, especially when it is autographed by you afterwards. The moment of connection is strongest after a concert, and a CD is a great way to further engage your followers.

Making an album not only takes a lot of time, but is also expensive. You need to think through how to finance your recording before you embark on the adventure. Crowdfunding has actually proven to be a great way to raise money for a recording, which we go into further detail on our crowdfunding chapter.

A day in a good studio costs between USD$1,000 to USD$3,000. For mixing and mastering, you then need to add around 50% to 100% of the recording times at a similar cost. For the manufacturing of the CD you will need to calculate between USD$1 to $2 when manufacturing a bigger batch of at least 500 units. Unfortunately, these costs do not even begin to cover any budgeting for graphic design, photography, writing and editing the booklet, marketing, or an EPK (electronic press kit). You can expect your recording project to start at USD$5,000 and easily cost up to USD$15,000.

However, when you feel ready for it at the right point in your career, we highly recommend recording an album. It still functions as one of the best calling cards you can have with promoters today, and should help you get more engagements. It is not a money-making opportunity, but has everything to do with opening more doors and opportunities, building your brand, and creating more followers.

[15]

TIME MANAGEMENT

AFTER SO MUCH DISCUSSION with regard to how you should manage your career, from social media, to sales and marketing, to sending out proposals and following up, one might wonder how one can fit all that into a single day. And yes, we should not forget that practicing and rehearsing should still take up the best part of your day.

Some might think that time and project management stand in contradiction to the creative processes necessary to create outstanding performances. To a certain extent, these objections might be right. However – and would you expect anything less here than an objection from us? - applied correctly, time and project management can boost the creative process and give it a more dedicated space than it would otherwise occupy.

With regard to time management, we want to address issues of your daily, weekly and monthly time allocation. Not only are we drawing from our own experiences, but we refer to many great time-tested management tools and books out there. With all the information available, everyone will develop his or her own unique time management strategy over time. Parts of it may differ greatly from what we advise, but regardless, we think it is important to start thinking of and developing an actual system as an important part of your career development.

Often there are days when we simply do not know where to start because we feel so stressed with all the work we should be doing. Then there are those days where there are no big concerts or other objectives coming up, so we do not know how to spend our time wisely and productively within a bigger picture.

SCENARIO PLANNING

We recommend breaking down your timelines into annual, weekly and daily time patterns and objectives. This can help focus your mindset and make you more productive.

A good starting point is the beginning of a year or the beginning of a season. Sit down with an old fashioned notebook – yes, that good old paper and pen! Start thinking about your goals, and in particular, your long term ones. What would you like to achieve in the next ten years? We have described this method in detail in the very first chapter CAREER STRATEGY but we think it is worthwhile coming back to it with a different twist, especially if you have jumped directly to this chapter. Try to put yourself in the ideal position of e.g. the year 2028 – so today, plus ten years. Describe your professional life, and perhaps your personal life as well, in that year. What would a typical day look like? What and where would you perform? How does this fit in with your personal life? Write down the answers to these questions, including detailed descriptions, in your notebook. Write it so clearly that anyone else reading it would be able to immediately picture you in that situation.

You might even ask your partner, mentor, teacher, coach, or a close friend, to really read it and tell it back to you. This exercise is not designed to judge what you wrote or to have the reader tell you how realistic your goals are. Rather, it is about sticking to the retelling of what you wrote down. This will help you to understand how clear your long-term vision is and where you might need to refine it.

For the second step, write down where you are today. Address similar questions of where and what you perform, how your personal life looks, etc. Stick to a fact-based detailed description of your current life. It certainly will look very different than the description of your situation ten years out. This might be a bit unsettling, but it is simply a part of the process of growth.

After writing these two scenarios down and perhaps discussing them with a trusted person, it is actually time to take a break. Go for a walk or sleep over these detailed word-paintings of your future and your current situation. These scenarios need to sink in, not only in your brain, but also in your emotions and your soul. Do not think about or judge them. Just let yourself be, and let your conscious and subconscious go to work.

After a good break, re-read both scenarios. Ask yourself how you feel about them and if you would like to make any changes with the descriptions. After reflecting on the scenarios, think about these three key questions:

- What does it take to get you from today's situation into your ideal scenario ten years out?

- What are the main obstacles on that path?

- What can you do to overcome these obstacles?

Again, write down the answers to these questions in as much detail as possible. Use full sentences and not just keywords, and use "action language." This means writing the answers to questions 1 and 3, stating what you will actively do, e.g. I will start addressing my stage fright by looking for a coach who can help me through this issue. Each sentence should start with "I will...".

Take another deep breath, or a walk, an espresso, a nap, whatever relaxes you. You have earned your break after going through this experience. If you do it right, it is actually exhausting, as you start questioning your whole life and thinking concretely about the future, and not only about your wishes, but about your concrete actions. This process might lead to an internal shift in your mindset and way of thinking.

Go back to your notebook and review your future scenario, your current situation, and the answers to the questions above. Now it is time to focus on the objectives for the coming twelve months. The idea is to generate between three to five objectives for the year, derived from the process above. Given this, you will need to prioritize the answers to your questions. Ask yourself not only what is most urgent to address, but also what can you best address given where you are now.

For example, if you are a young dramatic soprano, you might dream of singing Wagner in ten years. It would not make sense to study the big Wagner roles now. Your voice and your personality will need to develop until you are ready for such work. But it might make sense to start with music leading up to Wagner, and to also look after your physical fitness such that singing long phrases ten years later will come easy to you. Also, learning German might be a good idea.

When selecting these three to five objectives, again, write them down. But write them down in a way that the most desired outcome is clear. To stick with the above example, the objective is not to get physically fitter. You might reason that this is to help you with your breathing, but the goal is too vague. Rather, your objective will be to run for 10km without stopping. The reasoning behind this is simple – first, you have a concrete, measurable goal that you can work towards and tick off a year later. Second, understanding that endurance sports, specifically, will help you get closer to your ten-year scenario is significantly more concrete than just doing sports in general.

Another practical goal, especially for singers, might be to learn German. There are more opera houses in Germany based on population than in any other country in the world. Many singers therefore aspire to find work in Germany. Speaking German and being able to sing in German is helpful. Your goal in that respect is not only to learn German, but to get your B1 German language test done.

You should carry your twelve months' objectives with you wherever you go. Take a photo of your notebook pages if need be, and look at it every day on your smartphone or computer. It should not be "lost" in a notebook you open up just once a year.

When Bernhard went through this thought process in the early 1990's: "I had just finished a season at the Opera Studio of the Zurich Opera House in Switzerland, performing small roles with great artists including José Carreras, Agnes Baltsa, Jonathan Miller and many more. I started auditioning at smaller houses in Germany hoping to get a fixed contract. I was also singing concerts, recitals and some opera productions. After having travelled across Germany extensively in night trains and being to many towns I did not even know existed, I wondered where my future was. In the summer of 1995, I sang a recital at the beautiful Schloss Elmau in Bavaria. However, after that recital, I felt a need to sit down and think through my professional future. Without knowing the concept of scenario planning at that time, I was wondering if I would be happy singing at small and mid-sized opera houses somewhere in Germany in ten years. The answer was quickly very clear to me – I would not be happy. That was the moment that I decided to stop singing and pursued a career in management and tech instead."

Daily Routine

Before taking your twelve months' objectives and breaking them down into a weekly schedule, it is important to discuss a daily routine. In order to do this best, you first need to understand when the most productive times during the day are for you. This is different for everyone. Neither Bernhard nor Bettina are morning people, but Bernhard is generally most productive working before (a late) lunch. This is the time when he is able to focus best and stay on task, whereas Bettina prefers the early afternoon to get the most things done efficiently.

Ask yourself, during what time of the day are you able to really focus for hours? When are you most creative and productive? When do you get the biggest tasks requiring more intensive concentration done? Hopefully you are looking at a daily window of four to five hours.

Mark this slot every single (working) day in your diary as "My Time." If you use an electronic calendar, just repeat that four/five-hour window as an appointment for every working day. This is your sacred time. Switch off all distractions – no email, text, or message notifications. If possible, switch off your phone. Pianist Maria Radutu (www.hellostage.com/maria-radutu) for example, tells you on her voicemail that she is not available in the mornings, but that she will return your call in the afternoon, as her mornings are fully devoted to practice. There is nothing more important for your career than capitalizing on the time that you are most productive. There is nothing that should get in your way or take the focus off your goals, so stick to it and defend it as strongly as possible.

Of course we all know that reality dictates that there are meetings, rehearsals, travel schedules, etc. to contend with, which eat into our most productive times. But that is precisely why you should protect your productive time as sacred. Interruptions should be exceptions and not the rule.

Your daily routine will also include other regular slots. Take aside a bit of time for some physical exercise, even if it is only a 30-minute walk. Many find mediation and/or yoga helpful in their daily routines. Read daily. Don't read business or music related books, but fiction, poetry or anything that inspires you beyond your regular work. Have a coffee (or yes, a tea...) with a friend or partner.

Business related tasks will fill an important portion of your daily routine as well. Many musicians spend 30 minutes to even two hours every day following up on the business side of their career, answering emails and returning calls, being active on social media, etc. In today's society, people do expect you to come back to them within 24 to 48 hours. These are not the most fun tasks, nor do they contribute to your development artistically, but they are necessary cogs in the machine that keep your career going.

If you read through the above, you can see how quickly your day fills up. This can mean you may not have much time for meetings, or even just hanging out. However, your career requires focus, which should show in your daily routine. Be rigorous with your time during the week. A strict and well-balanced daily routine will not necessarily guarantee you a career as a successful musician, but missing one will definitely not get you there.

YOUR WEEKLY SCHEDULE

We recommend setting aside two hours on the same day every week to look back on the finishing week and plan the upcoming one. Bernhard usually does this on Friday mornings, although it can be shifted to Sunday evenings when he is traveling.

The starting point of any weekly planning session will be any fixed events like performances, rehearsals, or travel times, as well as your "My Time's" from your Daily Routine. First of all, make sure that you schedule in your performance routines and rest times before any performances. You should know your performance day routine and it should be non-negotiable. Everyone has their own routine from practicing for hours, to sleeping right up to the performance.

Now look at your twelve months' objectives and think which concrete tasks might help you get a step closer to your objective. Write this task down and plan it into your weekly schedule. If it has to do with your music, then you can use your "My Time" for it. If it has to do with other objectives, schedule it in around that time. Don't just add it to a long to-do list, but put the required time to achieve that task in as an "appointment" into your diary. This will enable you to really work on the task, as opposed to wondering what to do with a growing to-do list.

Try not to plan for more than six hours in a single day, including your "My Time", tasks from objectives, meetings, etc. You will still need the remaining time to deal with everything else that is going on around you, not to mention that sometimes things can run over, such as meetings. While it's not always possible to stick with the six hours of booked time a day, it is a good goal.

There are many jokes that musicians do not have a weekend. Nevertheless, we believe there is a reason why all major religions have a day of rest per week. So when planning your week, make sure you schedule at least one day "off." This really should be a completely free day, where you can enjoy the day doing whatever you like to do. It will refresh you and often bring new perspectives. We say this knowing that reality often gets in the way, and although you may not feel it as much when you are younger, excessively being "on" will eventually catch up to you. Carving out time for rest is an important rule you should set up early to take care of yourself into your future.

To-Do Lists

Many people create to-do lists. They tend to get longer, and longer, and longer. In our experience, there are a few things to consider.

First of all, there is a difference between tasks and to-do's. Tasks are directly related to your objectives and function as a step towards achieving your long-term goals. They take longer than a few minutes, so they therefore need to be added as an "appointment" in your diary so that you set enough time aside to do them.

To-do's on the other hand have a short time requirement. They are often about something simple, such as making an appointment with someone, returning a call, or some other such action. While they are important for your professional life, they are mostly reactive and will not necessarily bring you that much closer to achieving your objectives. Having them on a to-do list helps. This list should be synchronized across all your devices so that you can quickly tick them off.

To-do's should also have a due date. They are often linked to projects. Utilizing software or a system allowing you to link them to projects helps.

A good way to deal with to-do's is also to categorize them. Examples for categories could be "phone", "home", "computer"... When traveling and presented with spare time on a train or waiting at the airport, you might filter your to-do list by "phone" and work through your calling list quickly.

[16]

PROJECT MANAGEMENT

MUSICIANS ARE INTUITIVELY VERY good at project management. Because their concerts and performances are set well in advance with dates that cannot be changed, musicians are very used to working towards a hard deadline and ensuring they are well prepared to perform. Nevertheless, we found that it might be helpful to add a short chapter on project management, as a musician's life encompasses more than just live performances. You might branch out into new territories that cover projects such as making a recording or promoting a concert (or even a series!) yourself.

The only three key points you really need to remember from this chapter are that project management is about ensuring the delivery of a desired quality within a specific timeline and on a budget allocated for it. Got it? Ok, you can jump to the next chapter now.

Well, thanks for staying with us! We'll definitely expand a bit on these three points. Project management has its values, especially when it comes to delivering more complex projects like a recording or self-promoting a concert, but also when working with other musicians on a special performance.

DESIRED QUALITY

Discussing the term "desired quality" with any artist is a tough call. As artists, we all want to deliver an optimal performance. It is the continual artists' dilemma that one rarely reaches that pinnacle, but one is constantly working hard to come as close as possible.

When considering the desired quality of a musical performance or a recording in project management terms, we have to look at the entirety of the whole program.

It does not help if a musician practices only the first movement of one of three sonatas she is going to play in a concert. She may bring it to an amazing quality level, but if she does not work on all the other movements as well, obviously the overall quality suffers. In the pursuit of artistic quality, you will always want to give extra consideration to the parts of the program that are more challenging than the others, and focus on how you can ensure that the whole program is ready when it needs to be. Not only does this require smart planning of your practice routine, but also a constant adaptation depending on the progress that is made.

When working together in an ensemble, this becomes trickier. Some ensembles have a defined leader such as a conductor for orchestras or sometimes a first violinist in string quartets. But ensembles in our times tend to be less hierarchical. You should agree on a process of quality control and management before you actually start working together.

If working in an ensemble without a conductor, we would recommend learning about the rehearsal process of the Orpheus Chamber Orchestra in New York (www.hellostage.com/OrpheusNYC). The Orpheus Chamber Orchestra has actually never worked with a conductor. It has a unique process in working on its musical interpretation and quality. One person steps out of the orchestra for twenty to forty minutes in a rehearsal and takes on the role of a listening facilitator. This person does not take the role of a conductor, telling the orchestra what he or she wants to hear. Rather, this momentarily designated point person is a listener, who will ask questions to the orchestra as well as answer their questions. It is a unique respectful process, which is built upon a lot of trust, but also includes humor. There is a common understanding of the rehearsal efficiency. You can find videos about their rehearsal process online. These are worthwhile watching.

Understanding how a group like the Orpheus Chamber Orchestra works entails the willingness to approach projects from a bigger picture point of view from the start. Once a vision is agreed upon, it is much easier to then break down the process into a list of smaller steps, involving practice plans and details such as program notes or even a page-turner. When working together with a team, you will want to divide up who will be in charge of organizing what, so that everyone can take ownership and thus be invested in the whole of the project. To ensure a certain desired quality, you will want to plan starting with an overall view, then plotting against your given timeline.

TIMELINES

Delivering on time is often a much bigger challenge outside of the music world. Musicians are much more acclimated to time constraints. Musicians do not have the luxury of calling a few weeks before a concert and asking to postpone it. If worse comes to worst, one could of course cancel, but this is obviously not a great option and not something one can do often. Your time management is therefore essential (see also the chapter TIME MANAGEMENT).

When preparing a program for a concert or a recording, we strongly recommend that you map out - in detail - how and when to work on your program. It probably makes sense to write into your daily journal which pieces you want to focus on when, and block out the hours in your diary out for this work. Make sure to leave enough time for unforeseen circumstances. This could include needing longer rehearsals for a certain piece, maybe being called in to perform something in between, or perhaps someone in your group getting sick. Writing your schedule in block for block in your diary helps you visualize the roadmap ahead of you. It can also help you learn about your own practice process and make you more efficient for the future.

This same process goes for when you are organizing a concert or the recording yourself, in addition to having to prepare the musical content for it.

A good way to time out your big projects is to work backwards. Start with the day of the concert or recording, and then work your way backwards to your starting date, filling in all the details along the way that need to be completed. A good rule of thumb in goal setting is to always pad your parameters by at least 10% to if not 15%, as something will always pop up. This way, you don't get derailed or discouraged off of meeting your timeline and leave room for possible miscalculations. For example, if you foresee 20 hours of practice for one particular piece, we recommend budgeting 22-23 hours to account for potential interruptions.

When working in an ensemble, you will need to agree on a rehearsal schedule. Preparing that in detail is helpful so that everyone is on the same page. It requires every member to come well prepared to a rehearsal and each person can plan their own personal practice time accordingly. The same is true for any meetings you set regularly when preparing for an event within a group context. Everybody needs to know what their individual tasks are and when they have to deliver.

We have seen some amazingly structured conductors. Bernhard can remember the Austrian composer and conductor H.K. Gruber preparing for a rehearsal with the Vienna Philharmonic. Gruber had four rehearsals of three hours each with the orchestra. His work plan for the rehearsals was scheduled down to the minute, as this helped him rehearse a difficult contemporary program efficiently. It also generated a lot of good will from the orchestra towards Gruber for his well-structured rehearsals. Because of his respect, care and discipline, they accorded him the same, and suffice it to say that the performances were outstanding.

To ensure that you are keeping time with your schedule, it is good to regularly check your progress. This might happen at the end of a rehearsal when working with an orchestra, or in a short weekly meeting when working on a longer project. Even if you work on your own, sit down with yourself every week. Check your progress. Check if you were able to achieve what you wanted to in the daily allotted time slots you penciled in your diary. These checks will help you adapt your focus if needed, which will make it easier to stay within the time frame you allocated for the project.

BUDGET

When dealing with a self-promotion or a recording, apart from the timing, money is an equally crucial aspect to keep an eye on. Delivering a project on budget becomes especially important when more people are involved and they share the financial burden with you. A good project starts with not only planning the time necessary, but also realistically budgeting the money you will need.

Money can also be broken down by line items so that you can monitor your expenses. The timeline you created with all your necessary tasks will actually come in handy here as well. You can use your earlier prep work as a springboard for budgeting. It is always helpful if you are able to check your budget against people who have already done similar projects, especially if it is the first time you are undertaking such a project. They might be able to tell you about costs you may not have thought about yet, what realistic assumptions may be, and importantly, where you can save money. In case you don't know anyone like this, you can always reach out and post something on the Orange Board of HELLO STAGE, as several of the members have engaged in self-promoting a concert or have set up a recording themselves. You will be able to get advice for your part of the world, but maybe also learn some interesting inputs from different countries.

Just as with time allocation, it is always recommended to include a line for unforeseen costs in any budget. Depending on the project and how sure you are about having budgeted correctly, this line should be between 3% to 10% of all costs.

When you start the project, monitor all the invoices you get, write a budget line for each, and add them to the same spreadsheet you initially used to draw up the budget, so that you can compare your predictions with actual costs.

You should update your budget along the same lines like you monitor your progress on your timeline so that it becomes a natural part of your weekly meeting or project review. If you are working with others on a project, do it together with them. It is always important for everyone to know where one stands on money so that every team member can feel supported and accountable.

Even though it can be scary to embark on a new and big project, planning it well and monitoring it regularly makes it much easier to manage. And what would our artistic lives be without these crazy huge projects that inspire us so?

[17]

INTRODUCTION TO FINANCE

THINKING ABOUT FINANCE MIGHT not be the most exciting chapter when reading about your career as a classical musician, but it is very much a necessary one. Many musicians focus on making great music and booking the work – making money then becomes just a given if these things happen. In this chapter however, we'd like to introduce some basic financial concepts due to the particular nuances of being a musician. We highly recommend that you work on your specific details with an accountant and a tax advisor. Because accounting and taxation differ from country to country, it can become very complex. Taxes are an intricate issue already, and if you are performing in different countries, you will need a professional tax advisor who regularly works with artists on such details. Here, we can provide just a general overview so you have some awareness around the issue.

Our focus is on freelance musicians, or partly freelance musicians. Musicians employed by an orchestra or an opera house will normally receive a straight salary. Their taxes will mostly be handled via their employers, as long as there is not any additional income.

However, as soon as any additional income is received from teaching, playing solo, etc., the concept of this chapter will then also apply.

INTRODUCTION

There are a few basic terms you need to be familiar with, which we will explain in more detail later in this chapter. First of all, the best approach in terms of your financials is to separate your personal finances from your professional ones. Consider your professional side similar to a company. We also recommend that you make this distinction between your personal and professional finances everywhere. This includes creating separate bank accounts, credit cards, etc. This separation will make your accounting much easier.

- **Revenue:** Revenue is not equal to income! Revenue is all the money you receive for your professional freelance work. It is the money you invoice people for.

- **Cost:** Cost is all the money you spend in order to be able to receive said revenues. Cost does not include your personal spending.

- **Profit:** Profit is revenues minus cost. As a freelance musician, this profit is the income you declare on your income statement for tax purposes.

Early on, you should make it a habit of collecting any and all receipts which could be relevant for the purposes of keeping track of your costs. You will also want to keep track of the money you receive in relation to all contracts and agreements. Check with your accountant to see if your country requires you to keep hard copies or if you are able to collect and store everything electronically. There are many good software programs and apps which can make your life much easier with regard to this, such as Expensify (www.expensify.com) which will capture all your expenses.

What is the minimum you should keep track of?

- Your contracts and performance agreements: These are your agreements with orchestras, presenters and promoters. Many will provide you with their standard form for you to sign. Make sure you store it properly.

- Your invoices: Often presenters will ask you to invoice them for your performance. Create a standard form for an invoice on your computer and make sure that your accountant approves of it. Keep in mind that the regulations of what needs to be on an invoice will depend on the country you base your tax residency in. In any case, an invoice should include your name and address, your bank's details for payment, your applicable tax number(s), the date or period of performances and rehearsals, the name of the production, the address of the promoter or orchestra as well as their tax details, and the invoice number.

- Receipts: You should collect receipts for any money you pay in relation to your work, from your hotel bill to your taxi receipt. If in doubt whether you can use it or not, take it and discuss it with your tax advisor. Again, receipts require a certain format. In many countries they will have a line explaining the services or goods you purchased, a separate line for the VAT, the date you purchased the goods or services, the address of the merchant, a receipt number, and their tax information.

We will now discuss the different categories of revenue, cost and profit in more detail and then address the issue of taxes.

REVENUES

Where can you actually generate revenues as a performing artist? As we have explained before, you will most probably establish a portfolio career in today's world and become involved in various projects. Financially what this means is that you will have multiple sources of income, which is a great opportunity, but this will also make your accounting more complex.

First and foremost, you will hopefully receive performance fees. This is the money you will get performing as a musician. Instrumentalists are mostly paid per performance, which includes all rehearsals needed when playing with an orchestra. As a singer or conductor, this might be similar, but if you are hired for an opera production taking four to eight weeks for example, you might receive additional fees for the rehearsal period. Some opera houses still pay a flat rehearsal fee, even for just a few days, while an opera-in-concert is mostly dealt with like a concert performance.

As a composer, you will rarely get performance fees directly from the venue unless you also conduct or perform your piece. Some orchestras may pay a small fee for you to attend the final rehearsals to ensure that the piece is performed in the way you intended it, in case this is the first performance in the country or they have not been part of the original commission agreement.

A commission agreement will get the composer a fee for a new piece. This might be with just one venue or orchestra/ensemble/soloist, or a few of them might group together to come up with the funds.

Many musicians teach. If you have a contract with a university, college or music school, the institution will take care of many aspects, but you will still need to calculate all the income you have received nevertheless in your annual tax declaration. If teaching privately, any money you receive from students should be treated as revenue.

We recommend that you get paid via bank transfer, PayPal, credit card or any other means, but not in cash. This makes the transaction easier to capture for your accounting purposes and more transparent for the tax authorities.

If you have recorded an album or your concert has been broadcast on radio or television, you might be entitled to royalties. You might get a fee for the recording itself. Sometimes it is included as part of your performance contract, but sometimes it is extra. If you maintain copyrights, you might be entitled to royalties from the sale of albums, downloads, broadcasts, etc. In many countries, royalties are handled by certain royalty-collecting societies. Don't forget to claim them as many of these societies sit on quite a bit of money they would very much like to distribute, but don't know how to get in touch with the performers.

Royalties are especially important for composers. Composers receive money whenever their music is performed. If you have a publisher, they will take care of royalties. More and more composers are now working without a publisher. If this is the case, you should get in touch with your national royalty-collecting association to understand what you need to do in order to receive said royalties.

Another source of revenues related to recording is licensing fees. If your recording is used for films, video clips, video games, or in another context, you are eligible for licensing fees as long as you maintain the relevant copyrights. Some of these fees will be collected by your royalty-collecting society. There is also an increasing number of internet platforms where you can upload samples which might get picked up by filmmakers or video game creators, and you can get paid for that separately.

Neither royalties nor licensing are huge sources of income for musicians, but they might just be a nice addition to your income.

There are many other sources of income for musicians. Many countries provide an array of subsidies and/or support for their artists. These include scholarships to study or to do master classes. They can be project specific. Often public bodies will subsidize the performance of contemporary music, especially from that country. Many countries also have organizations to support the export of music, providing you with subsidies to perform abroad, attend important conferences, or spend time composing in a different country. Many countries have cultural representations abroad like the British Council or the German Goethe Institute or have cultural attachés in their embassies. They are always looking for performers in their venues abroad. While their budgets are often small, the additional revenue might help you procure an additional performance in a country you were touring anyway, or provide you with funding for international airfare, allowing you to perform in more venues in that country. We would encourage you to research these opportunities, and speak to the people and associations and apply.

Various companies have sponsorship programs for young musicians around the world. They provide them with bursarship to study or to do master classes, performance opportunities, and support for their projects. Again, researching who actually supports artists in your community and country is a good starting point. See who has dedicated programs that you can apply to.

Many charitable foundations support artists and classical music. Although they are often hard to find, there are some directories of foundations online or available as printed directories.

All over the world, private individuals support artists. Again, though it is hard to find such people, asking around, seeing where your friends perform, and going to house concerts might help you to identify these people. Sometimes they will also just find you. The process of getting supported by private individuals often takes longer, as building up trust first is crucial. But we have seen many private donors who have supported artists even through their most difficult times.

The last few years, crowdfunding has become a totally new source of revenue for artistic projects and musicians. It is so important that we actually devote a whole chapter to it in this book. Make sure that you check the tax treatment of any income you receive via crowdfunding with your tax advisor before starting your campaign. Because crowdfunding is so new, tax legislation often has not caught up with it yet.

Composers have a special revenue opportunity through commissions. Commissions to write a new piece of music can come from multiple sources – from public bodies to private individuals and other musicians. When composers are well established, the amount they get paid for the commission depends on if they are writing for a solo instrument, a small ensemble, or a large orchestra, and on how long the piece is. Yes, composers get paid by the minute – kind of.

Cost

As mentioned before, costs include all expenditures related to your professional activities. Money spent on your personal needs cannot be included in this accounting for your professional career, and there are often more costs related to your professional life than you might realize. We will go through some of them here.

The most obvious costs involve travel, getting to and from performances and rehearsals. These can include airfares, train tickets, taxi rides, car hire, hotel bills and more. In some countries, there is a rate per kilometer driven in your private car that can be recognized as costs for tax purposes. Some countries also allow you to add a per diem rate to your travel costs for tax purposes, again reducing your tax burden. Do check with your tax advisor in order to understand the specific regulations in your country. One caveat we should mention is when combining private and professional travel - this often requires splitting costs fairly between private and business purposes.

The renting of a rehearsal room or studio is often recognized as costs. This might even include a dedicated room in your apartment that you use for practice. Musicians need to rehearse and practice; it is a regular part of conducting business. The same rule can apply towards an office or office space. Be aware that tax authorities might check if the rooms you use for professional purposes really are only used for said purposes.

Costs include everything around your instrument, from repair to maintenance to insurance. Purchasing an instrument is a special case and falls under capital expenditure, which we will address later. Also, scores, office material, etc. should be included in costs. Anything around the management aspects of your career, from the cost of an internet connection, hosting, to phone bills, etc. are considered to be costs in your accounting. Also included would be professional fees you pay to lawyers and accountants, as well as membership fees for professional associations.

Costs related to the marketing of your career should be considered in your accounting. This includes printing fees for business cards and flyers, travels cost to meetings, and sometimes even meals, which have a clear business purpose, and similar marketing related expenditures.

Some tax legislations allow recognize concert clothing as costs for tax purposes. This should definitely be kept within reason and it is good to check with your tax advisor, but if your tails or evening gown is mostly really only used for performances, you might be able to consider this a cost.

CAPITAL EXPENDITURE

Capital expenditures are separate from costs. Simply put, when you purchase something of value that you will use over a longer period, it is usually not considered a cost, but an investment or a capital expenditure. This has an impact on your taxation, because for tax purposes, only a small part of the purchase price of an item is considered as cost in the year of purchase. Actually, the same amount will be seen as cost for tax purposes over a period of several years, in a process called depreciation.

For musicians, capital expenditure mostly occurs in two cases – when buying an instrument, and when buying computer or tech equipment. Buying an instrument is often a very big – and quite expensive – step for musicians. Violins, more often than not, are the most expensive instruments, with prices sometimes reaching millions of dollars. But pianos, different arrays of percussion instruments, and so on, also cost a lot of money.

Before purchasing an instrument, you will need to think about how to finance them, meaning how to procure the funds to pay for them. Perhaps you are in a lucky position where you have enough to pay for them, or you might be able to trade in your current instrument to partially cover your costs, which is great. Many musicians however, often need to take out a bank loan or find someone to help support them in the purchase.

For valuable instruments (mainly string instruments), there are foundations that purchase instruments and loan them to musicians. However, the conditions of these agreements differ widely. Check with other musicians playing an instrument from any given foundation to see if this is a viable option for you. Some of the conditions of these loan agreements to consider are:

- How long are you allowed to play this instrument?

- What happens at the end of the loan period? Can you renew the contract or will you lose the instrument?

- What happens if the foundation decides to sell the instrument? Can you keep it for a certain period? Could you buy it from them if you can finance it? Or do you have to return it quickly?

- Who pays for the insurance and could you afford to pay for it?

- How often and where do you have to show the instrument to an instrument maker? Who pays for these checks and the travel?

- Can you travel freely with this instrument?

If you travel with your instrument, please make sure that you have all the proper paperwork with you. This can be quite a lot of work and sometimes tedious, but it should include among other things: a certificate of ownership, a proof of you being allowed to travel with and play the instrument, and a statement of the materials used in it from a certified expert. Find out if any of the materials used are on a non-import or non-export list, such as ivory, and where, if at all, you can travel with it. We have heard all too often from musicians where their instruments, or a bow, was seized by customs in various countries.

Other capital expenditures include computers or technical equipment. For tax purposes here, they are mostly depreciated over time, meaning that only part of the purchase cost can be included in your annual tax declaration.

Taxes

We are certainly not tax experts and you are strongly advised to find and work with an experienced tax advisor in your own country of residence. We will provide you with a few questions you should ask them:

- Sales tax: Sales tax or value added tax (VAT) has to be paid for any goods or services sold. This means that you might need to add VAT to any invoices you send out for your services, including performing, teaching, etc. Many tax legislations have a certain threshold under which you do not need to pay VAT. Check that threshold with your tax accountant. When paying VAT, you can offset VAT you paid for yourself.

- Income tax: Whether you want to or not, you will need to pay income taxes at some point. What many freelancers forget is that these payments are often due up to over one year later than when you received the associated money. It would be prudent to set aside into a separate account any money you will roughly owe for tax and social security payments whenever you receive revenues. This will avoid nasty surprises when a big tax bill arrives on your doorstep.

- Many countries now exercise withholding taxes for artists who performed in their country but are not resident there. These are normally paid directly by the promoter or whoever engaged you to the tax authorities, thereby reducing the money you should expect to receive according to your contract. Find out early from the person who sent you the contract, if and what kinds of withholding taxes apply, and what the exemptions are. If withholding taxes are deducted, ensure that you have the proper paper work for your accountant to include that in your tax declaration. Withholding taxes already paid in other countries should lower your income tax burden.

- Social security: Although, technically speaking, this is not a tax, we add it to this section. Many countries require you to pay for social security, and often you pay much later. These payments can often show up as an unwanted surprise, so make sure your paperwork is in order and you have money set aside for such payments.

INSURANCE

We'd like to add a brief section on insurance to add to this chapter on finances, especially since young people often do not really think about the necessities of getting insurance. In some countries, social security costs might provide you with the basic safety net you need.

There are four types of insurances you need to think of:

- Health insurance: Everyone can get sick. Doctors and hospitals can quickly become unaffordable. Make sure that you have suitable health insurance that can also cover you while abroad. Freelancers have to deal with the big disadvantage of not only having to pay their medical bills, but also not earning any money while ill.

- Invalidity insurance: Musicians need their hands, their fingers, their voice, etc. to be able to perform and earn money. Any permanent or chronic damage to your body can endanger your whole career and your money-making potential. You therefore should have insurance that would pay you some money in a worst case scenario, allowing you to re-school and start again.

- Pension and retirement: The day will come when you will stop performing. It might be ages away, but thinking about it early enough allows you to plan for it with very little money.

- Instrument: Your instrument is the second most important part of you performing. Therefore, make sure it is properly insured and that you can replace it should anything happen to it.

A chapter on finances and insurance is probably not the most exciting one in a book about managing your career so thank you if you've read all the way through till here. We do hope that we had some helpful tips for you in this chapter to help you to take care of the financial side of your business in a better and more informed way.

[18]

LAST WORD

AFTER ALL THESE PAGES writing about business, management, money and other things, we do want to encourage you to go out there and make great music. We cannot wait to see and hear you on stage!

ABOUT THE AUTHORS

BERNHARD KERRES

Bernhard Kerres fell in love with classical music starting in early childhood. Living in Vienna, he was brought up with the Vienna Philharmonic and the Vienna State Opera. He started his career as an opera singer and sang, among other places, in the studio of the Opera Zurich with José Carreras, Agnes Baltsa and others. Later following his interest in technology, he joined the strategy consulting firm Booz & Co after his MBA at London Business School. From there he was recruited into C-level positions of two large European tech firms. He served on the board of classical music institutions and advised them before he was named CEO and Artistic Director (Intendant) of the Wiener Konzerthaus in 2007, which he led for six years. In 2013, he followed his dream combining his passion for classical music with his fascination for technology, and founded HELLO STAGE, the largest classical music community online.

Bernhard was awarded the Austrian Cross for Science and Art and the Chilean Bernardo O'Higgins Order. Bernhard regularly speaks and publishes on innovation, entrepreneurship and leadership.

BETTINA MEHNE

Bettina Mehne descends from a violin maker's family in Berlin. She studied musicology and history of Art alongside working in the offices of the Deutsche Symphonie-Orchester Berlin and the Berliner Festwochen. Upon graduation, she joined the touring department of Harrison Parrott in London. In 1999, she opened the German office of Van Walsum Management within the Konzertdirektion Schmid before joining Die Deutsche Kammerphilharmonie Bremen in 2001 as their Artistic Manager. Having headed the artistic planning at the Wiener Konzerthaus for six seasons, Bettina left at the end of the 2012/13 season together with the then Intendant Bernhard Kerres to cofound with him the new venture HELLO STAGE.